E

Meeting the Early Learning Goals through Role Play

A practical guide for teachers and assistants

MARIE ALDRIDGE

David Fulton Publishers
London

David Fulton Publishers Ltd
The Chiswick Centre, 414 Chiswick High Road, London W4 5TF

www.fultonpublishers.co.uk

First published 2003

10 9 8 7 6 5 4 3 2 1

British Library Cataloguing in Publication Data
A catalogue record for this book is available from the British Library.

ISBN 1 84312 036 4

Typeset by BookEns Ltd, Royston, Hertfordshire
Printed and bound in Great Britain by Ashford Colour Press Limited, Gosport, Hants

CONTENTS

ACKNOWLEDGEMENTS

I wish to thank:

all the children I have worked with at Banks Road School, who have constantly inspired me with their imagination and enthusiasm. In particular those children (and their parents) who have permitted me to use photographs in this book;

my head teacher Mrs Susan Devereux who is committed to the development of socio-dramatic and thematic role play for all our children;

Liverpool Early Years Development Team for their role in my professional development. In particular, lecturer Anita Ryall and her colleague Irene Travis, for their great expertise and support;

colleagues from school, Anne, Jennette, James, Linzi, Annetta, Andrea and Joan, Vicki and Jean, with whom I have really enjoyed working. I appreciate all their encouragement, support and enthusiasm towards all our new projects;

David Fulton Publishers, particularly Nina Stibbe, for their professional guidance through the writing process;

and my family: husband Barry for his confidence in me and patience, Clare for her practical support and Michael for his technical photographic expertise and my friend Jane Bentham for her invaluable assistance with the final draft.

INTRODUCTION

Children need pretend play not as a treat but as a right.
(Hendy and Toon 2001)

The inclusion of all reception children in the foundation stage (QCA 2000) has encouraged practitioners to appreciate the importance of play in young children's development. Role play is a major component of this play and encourages them to act out real-life and fantasy scenarios to develop their imaginative skills independently.

A large number of early learning goals can be experienced using themed role play topics, which, if planned and organised successfully, can allow learning opportunities in all of the six areas identified by QCA (2001): personal, social and emotional development; communication, language and literacy; mathematical development; knowledge and understanding of the world; physical development; and creative development. These are then subdivided by QCA into developmental stepping stones which finally build up to reach the learning goal and beyond.

This book evolved as a tool for the foundation stage to use in our school to develop socio-domestic and thematic role play. It takes the six areas of learning and offers suggestions on how some of these may be covered.

One of the preconceived ideas of any role play is that the equipment required will be expensive, but this is false, as good role-play activities can occur using only simple sets, a few free and available resources and effective adult support.

This book places its emphasis on the use of cheap everyday materials to develop different themes and storing them so they can be reused at a later date. The children and staff started by collecting basic domestic play props together and the children began to play with them. The scope and intensity of their play was magnificent, as they created their own scenarios, acted out events and became aware of different activities relating to different times of the day. My colleagues encouraged the children to take the lead in their play so staff would only be in supportive roles and not control it.

The unintrusive presence of adults enhances pretend play and can increase the duration of play.
(O'Connel and Bretherton 1984)

We tried to introduce scope for some progression in play between nursery and reception. Nursery already had some themed activities and we wanted to extend them into reception making them more challenging and advanced with play scenarios showing some progression of dramatic skills. These grew from strength to strength as everyone involved became more and more enthusiastic.

The team including the children chose each of the themed topics, and then opportunities for learning from the stepping stones were identified. We discussed ideas with the children and took some of their ideas on board. We put them on grids to make them easily accessible and show a way that each theme can be developed, respecting the children's contributions.

> *Children do like to be asked by adults to share their experiences of the development of the role-play area and not have the adults create it for them.*
>
> (Smith 1999)

The importance of play is not a new phenomenon but was recognised in the early twentieth century by Susan Isaacs who developed a child development department in London; she thought that children learnt best if allowed to play and investigate things. She encouraged her children to fantasise and be creative with their own ideas. Others followed such as Vygotsky, who felt that children could play together and bring their thinking forward.

A more current expert, Tina Bruce, feels that play helps children to develop their intelligence in every way and has developed an observational method which may be employed to record effective play (see Appendix). She developed 12 indicators, which if observed help to indicate the quality of real play taking place.

> *In order to increase our knowledge of play and develop practice wisdom we need to become skilled and effective observers of play.*
>
> (T. Bruce 2001)

We practised and developed our observational skills using photographs, tapes and written observational notes (often sticky notes) and began to develop a system of utilising this information to help future planning and monitor individual children's development. These assessments have always been important and have recently become a compulsory section of the New Pupil Profiles (QCA 2002) which will come into operation in summer 2003.

In developing countries children still use symbolic play, but it is often the result of oral stories that reflect the culture in which they live. Our society has become very influenced by technology with lots of domestic and manual jobs done by machines and computers. These are often very difficult scenarios for children to recreate in the classroom.

It is our job as practitioners to give them the opportunity to experience all types of social-dramatic and thematic play. These I strongly feel are both effective tools to deliver the foundation stage curriculum, which should not be subject-based but should be a holistic curriculum which develops the whole child. The curriculum should prepare them for our ever-changing world through non-threatening scenarios, allowing them to be toolmakers and cultural thinkers, facilitating development of the skills needed for life and learning.

I hope this book will prove useful to all early years practitioners as an implement to initiate role play where it does not exist and to enhance programmes that are already running.

HOUSE

Home area

Play situation

Create a home area that reflects the children's own homes, so that they can readily identify with it and feel confident to play inside it. The area should exhibit some features of each child's home and can gradually be modified during the year by adding additional equipment and celebrating special events, e.g. birthday celebrations, moving house, family outings or holidays: Christmas, Chinese New Year etc. (See Tables 1–9.)

Introductory prompts

Where do you live?
Who lives in your house?
How many rooms are there in your house?
Are all the rooms the same?
How are they different?
Which room do you cook a meal in?
Where do you keep the food?
Where do you have a bath?
Where do you sleep?
What happens in the living room?

Possible roles

Family members: Mum, Dad, Grandpa, Grandma, children, babies, aunts and uncles and friends. Household visitors: milkman, postman, grocer, removal person, estate agent, characters for celebrations etc.

Resources

Supply your home area with furniture, cooking equipment, tea sets, dinner sets, multicultural cooking and eating equipment, dressing-up clothes, hairdryers, vacuum cleaners, cleaning equipment, place mats, washing and drying machines, clothes horse or washing line, iron and ironing board, beds, bathroom equipment and dolls of different kinds. Provide a car for shopping, outings etc., removal van, books, magazines, labels, diaries, directories, notices, message board, note pads, shopping lists, booklets, notebooks, writing tools, telephones, TV, tape recorder and radio.

Have some household items with numbers on: cookers, telephones, clocks, computers, videos, magazines and catalogues etc. that all use the numbers for a variety of functions including price, time, distance and identification. A selection of real objects can be matched and sorted depending on a variety of criteria: colour, size, type and pattern. Another group of real objects can be provided to explore the concepts of position: cups, saucers, spoons, knives, forks, soft toys, dolls, large toys.

See Recommended reading for books to use for the home area.

Link activities

Decorate the house.
Create different rooms using self-made equipment.
Make family portraits for the wall.
Think about their own homes and discuss similarities and differences.
Discuss household activities and try to recreate them in the role play house.
Plan a birthday party or another special event.
Plan a holiday or outing and discuss what they may need to do and buy.
Think about moving house and the people who may become involved.

Potential learning opportunities

Personal, social and emotional development

The home area helps children to:

Disposition and attitude

- explore new learning experiences in a familiar setting with the area constantly growing and developing at their request;
- initiate play and build upon their own personal interests, experiences and ideas of their homes to solve problems that arise in the role-play home;
- enjoy themselves with their friends and supporting adults and begin to reflect on their play experiences;

Self-confidence and self-esteem

- improve their confidence and begin to develop their own personal character and personality;

Making relationships/behaviour/self-control

- express feelings and be sensitive to the needs of others;
- develop relationships with children showing respect, interest and care for others (families and friends);
- share the limited space fairly so that their play can develop, they can take turns, develop self-made rules of behaviour and improve their ability to work as members of a group;

Self-care

- develop an awareness of their own personal needs: washing, toileting, getting dressed etc. through play;
- try to tackle new problems, e.g. tying laces, zipping up coats, fastening buttons, and begin to feel proud of their own achievements through play;
- feel confident to ask for help from a familiar adult or peer when problems arise or equipment is not available;
- select appropriate equipment for a task and use it sensibly;

Sense of community

- appreciate that others have different customs, beliefs, gender, race and ability and have respect and empathy for them by offering equal opportunities within all learning experiences involved with homes;
- begin to have a more detailed understanding of the community they live in by looking firstly at their own homes and family, and then moving out into the community with photographs, stories and visitors.

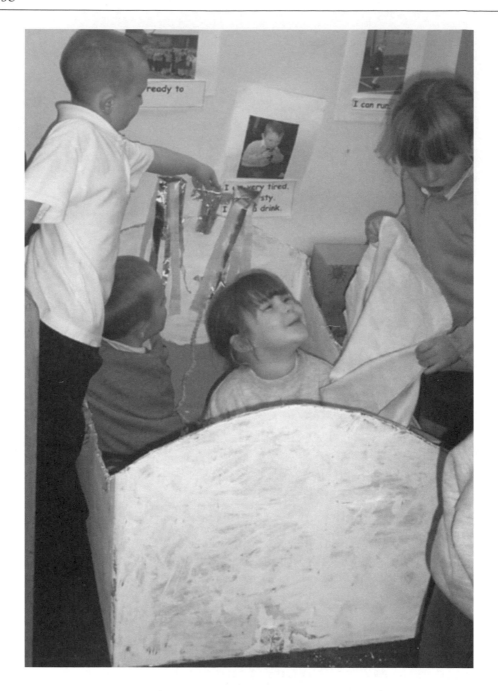

Communication, language and literacy

The home area helps children to:

Speaking, listening and communicating

- speak clearly and use appropriate body language to get attention, to defend their own interests and to be understood by friends and family;
- name everyday objects about the house and develop their language skills using adjectives to describe them in simple sentences;

- begin to use language as a means of communicating: giving simple instructions, asking for help and expressing opinions;
- develop questioning techniques using how, when, where and why;

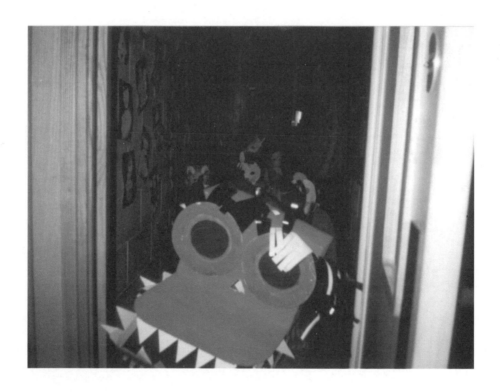

- respond to and use appropriate social conventions such as please and thank you;
- use their language skills to take on and recreate family roles and familiar experiences;

Reading and linking sounds to letters

- develop the need to be able to read by having a large selection of household printed materials around for them to use freely (packets, recipes, newspapers, magazines, posters, maps, catalogues, mail, class-made reading materials, e.g. zig-zag books, leaflets) so that they understand writing carries meaning;
- begin to identify printed materials such as birthday cards, letters and phone books;
- use household equipment and become familiar with how it works, e.g. microwave, telephone, tape recorder, television, video and computers;

Writing

- experiment with mark-making tools and materials in the home area;
- begin to recognise and write their own name, friends' names and other familiar words, recording messages, writing letters and cards, form filling and writing cheques.

Mathematical development

The home area helps children to:

Matching and sorting

- match and sort real objects around the house according to size, colour, shape and other criteria;
- put toys away in appropriately labelled places;
- sort objects according to function, e.g. clothes to wear outside;

Matching/ordering

- recognise and continue patterns on materials or wallpaper;

Number

- match, recognise and write numbers around the home, e.g. on cookers, videos, catalogues;
- recognise personal numbers and their significance, e.g. birthdays, house numbers etc.;
- count objects accurately around the house and to develop an ability to estimate;

Calculations

- begin to investigate simple practical calculations involving addition and taking away using real objects around the house. To begin to solve real problems,

e.g. 'Have we enough biscuits?' 'How many red and green plates are there altogether?;
- begin to compare two sets of familiar household objects using mathematical language such as more, less and the same as;

Shape, space and measure

- find different 2-D and 3-D shapes in the house and the environment;
- discuss similarities and differences introducing mathematical language, e.g. flat, curved, straight, using equipment like bottles and boxes;
- begin to use shapes in planning and creating new environments such as television, wallpaper, telephones, windows etc. made from boxes and other throwaway materials;

Size/area/length/capacity/weight

- begin to think about size and the language related to it, e.g. big, little, tall, short etc. and introduce the tools used for measuring length;
- understand the concept of weight during everyday role-play activities, e.g. the heaviest doll, food or bricks, and to begin to use the appropriate language for measuring weight;
- use capacity in the house and to be able to use the appropriate vocabulary including full and empty, e.g. bottle of milk, empty cup and spoonful of sugar etc;

Time

- discuss times of the day when different household activities occur: meals, bedtime and showers etc. and begin to develop a sequence of events, e.g. getting dressed;
- begin to use the names of the days of the week and times on the clock.

Knowledge and understanding of the world

The home area helps children to:

Observe/explore/classify

- have an interest in and display curiosity about their environment and bring ideas back from their own homes;
- sort and classify objects and materials both natural and man-made found about the home;

Materials and their properties

- explore, recognise and describe the properties and uses of different materials;
- talk about household appliances that use electricity and be aware of the dangers. To compare the advantages with manual methods, e.g. washing machines;

- gain an awareness of the fact that force and energy are required to cause movement (petrol, food);
- identify sources of environmental sounds, e.g. vehicles, dogs, telephones;
- know where light comes from in the house: light sources, reflections and shadows;
- know what clothes to wear in different kinds of weather and how we change them during the year;

Design and making

- design and make equipment for the house, e.g. beds for dolls, wallpaper, clocks, television and washing machine and to be able to use a variety of tools and materials;
- design and make a trolley to move large items from one place to another using large construction kits;

ICT

- recognise and investigate the use of ICT in the role-play house and their own homes;
- use the CD-ROM SEMERC Microworlds 2000 (Granada Learning Ltd.) to develop their knowledge of homes;

A sense of place

- look at their own homes and record what they see in pictorial form and use this information to compare them and modify the role-play area;

- look at non-fiction books and videos and investigate how people live in other lands and compare their homes and facilities (igloos, tents, palaces, houseboats) through play;

A sense of time

- understand what homes were like long ago. Use stories (e.g. *Peepo!*) and explore real old household items to bring alive the past.

Creative development

The home area helps children to:

Exploring media and materials

- make props for the role-play house, e.g. wallpaper and box television, using a wide selection of resources;
- make a set of window scenes to reflect the changing seasons;
- paint family portraits and take photographs around the home corner;

Music

- recreate sounds and music that they are familiar with in the home, e.g. telephone, dishwasher, vacuum cleaner, radio, television, CD, by using a tape recorder;
- listen to familiar music that is played in their homes, e.g. themes from television and radio programmes;
- learn songs and rhymes related to the home (see Recommended reading);

Imagination

- use the props available to support their role play effectively and act out roles to represent real scenarios in the home;
- understand how one familiar object can be used to represent another, e.g. ruler for a spoon;
- engage in sequenced role play, e.g. pretend to make a cup of tea;
- cooperatively play to act out an invented story based around the home, e.g. moving house;
- use the house to act out familiar stories, sometimes extending the characters.

Physical development

The home area helps children to:

Movement

- explore the way they move and learn to take care when moving from one area to another, e.g. stairs;

Sense of space

- explore the idea of personal space by fitting themselves into confined spaces and making new dens out of blankets and boxes;
- develop an awareness of the needs of others to have space to move about in;
- use directional and positional language in relation to real situations in the home: when they place furniture or tell guests where to sit;

Health and bodily awareness

- encourage healthy living with play situations in the house: eating fruit and taking exercise;

Using tools and equipment

- use large and small equipment safely with increased control and coordination: moving house;
- improve their own skills and control over clothes and simple fastenings when they dress up.

Key vocabulary

house, roof, walls, bricks, rooms, bedroom, kitchen, bathroom, living room, hall, garden, shed, floor, carpets, tiles, lino, wooden, wallpaper, paint, furniture, chairs, tables, cupboards, beds, wardrobes, drawers, toilet, bath, shower, stairs, doors, sink, washer, dryer, dishwasher, fridge, freezer, cooker, microwave, food mixer, vacuum cleaner, hair dryer, clothes, kitchen equipment, pretend and real food, shopping, family members, buy, sell, money, estate agent, removal van, pack

Extended play situations

You could extend the role play in the home area using these ideas.
Create different rooms for different functions.
Wash hands using different soaps, brushes and creams, to know the sequence of how they wash their hands and to know when and why they need to wash their hands.
The children care for their teeth by brushing twice a day in the bathroom. Try different kinds of toothpaste and see which is their favourite. What colour and type of toothbrush do they use? Sequence the order of cleaning their teeth.
Bath dolls using shampoo to wash dolls' hair. Explain the importance of keeping their hair clean.
Explain the importance of going to bed and having enough sleep. They bring in their pyjamas and pretend to go to bed and wake up in the role-play area.
They try cooking and making drinks for themselves (cocoa, milkshakes and cakes), measuring, pouring and using special tools, e.g. food-mixer.
They dress and undress, using fastenings, turning clothes from being inside-out, using dolls as well as themselves to understand the sequence of dressing.
Discuss the importance of keeping fit, active and exercise as they develop hobbies and enjoy playing active games with their friends.
Talk about the members of their family and how all families are different; how babies grow and need different care to adults; how it is important to share all the jobs around the house (equal opportunities) and help each other.
Discuss moving house and all that is involved with selling and buying houses.

Observational focus

Observe children informally and later ask them a variety of questions. Give them simple problem-solving situations connected to activities that happen in the house, and assess how they answer and solve them.

1. Cannot remember any significant information/detail ☐
2. Can remember a small amount of information/detail ☐
3. Can give a full account of how various activities in the house are carried out ☐
4. Can extend their play by creating new characters and scenarios ☐

Table 1   Kitchen and dining room

Date	Role play	House: Kitchen and dining room	
	Com./lang./lit. development	Mathematical development	Other areas of development
1	Discuss how to set up the area as an imaginary kitchen. What do the children think they will need? Rules that apply when they play. Number of children and roles they can play: mums, dads, children, friends and family. What we can do in this area.	Use shape, colour and texture to create a new area. Think about the size of the items. Think where numbers are useful in the home and display them.	Make props, create kitchen and living room. Discuss the safety of using certain appliances (electrical). Play, listen and communicate with one another.
2	What props they think they may need to make and what they have already got. **Kitchen:** cooker, sink, washer, dryer, fridge, microwave, kitchen equipment, tea set, plates, pans, knives, forks, spoons etc. **Dining room:** chairs, table, tablecloth.	Store tools and equipment with silhouettes to help keep the kitchen tidy. Set the table, matching items by colour and size.	Table manners and eating politely. Communicating with each other around the table. Personal hygiene and food hygiene. Washing up in hot soapy water. Compare drying equipment (dishwashers VS. tea towels).
3	Collect and make food props to create meals. Add cookbooks and recipe cards. Use food-mixers to	Weigh ingredients using spoonfuls, scales, tools. Measure liquids using a spoon and measuring jug.	Importance of polite behaviour when talking and working with people. Respect what others say and listen

Table 1 *(Contd)*

Date	Role play	House: Kitchen and dining room	
	Com./lang./lit. development	Mathematical development	Other areas of development
	help you cook. Follow instructions. Cook in ovens and microwave (compare).		carefully to them. Jobs certain family members do encouraging equal opportunities and reducing stereotyping.
4	Act out different meal scenarios. Compare the types of food we eat at different meals.	Think of the times of the day, different meals at different times of the day: breakfast, lunch, tea, supper.	Use real food and allow the children to create real meals following recipes and verbal instructions. Share the food out when cooked.
5	Listen to cooking stories and rhymes and try acting them. Pat a cake, The Queen of Hearts, etc.	Make sandwiches, cakes and tarts and count them. Look at their shapes. Use real food and dough.	Play with new equipment that has been made. Can they make suggestions on how it can be improved by playing, communicating and working together?

Table 2 Living room

Date	Role play	House: Living room	
	Com./lang./lit. development	Mathematical development	Other areas of development
1	Discuss setting up the area as an imaginary living room with them and decide what they need (armchairs, sofa, carpet, TV and video), think about rules that might apply, and the possible roles: mums, dads, children, friends and family. What can we do in the area?	Make sure you have enough chairs for each family member, high chair for baby.	Start to make props for area. Decorate chairs and make a sofa using cushions and brightly coloured fabric.
2	Think about all the electronic items in your living room. Discuss what they do.	Look at the numbers on electronic items and record where you find them. Why are the numbers there, e.g. channels, volume, power etc.?	Make some electronic props out of boxes, e.g. TV, video, CD, computer, play station.

Table 2   *(Contd)*

| Date | Role play | House: Living room | |
	Com./lang./lit. development	Mathematical development	Other areas of development
3	Read *What's the Time Mr Wolf?* Discuss what activities you do in the living room at different times of the day. Look at time rhymes, e.g. Hickory Dickory Dock.	Count around the clock, match numerals and make observational pictures of different types of clocks, writing down the numbers. Look at other ways of measuring time (timers). Activities completed in 1 minute.	Make large grandfather clock. Make mice to go up and down. Discuss activities you do at different times of the day and act out.
4	Discuss with the children what their family did last night. Did they play games, watch the TV, read a book, paper, comic, write a letter, etc.? Read *Peepo!* (big book) and investigate how families entertained themselves. Compare with today.	Look at simple card games (pairs, snap), dominoes and board games where dice and counting are involved. Did the children enjoy playing them?	Play complex computer-based games. Think of how often you talk to each other. Did the children enjoy playing them? Compare to simple board and card games.
5	Think about how houses are cleaned. What would they use in past times and what do Mum and Dad use now?	Time cleaning activities using counting, stopwatch etc. and record what you find out.	Compare cleaning tools today and in the past: brooms, dustpan and brush, mops to vacuum cleaners and carpet cleaners. Compare the time and how well the jobs are done.

Table 3 Family celebration

Date	Role play	House: Family celebration	
	Com./lang./lit. development	Mathematical development	Other areas of development
1	Discuss making props and materials we would need to gather for a family celebration. What roles could the children take on? Make and send party/celebration invitations.	Predict the number of guests coming to the party. Begin to get the correct number of resources ready. Count candles etc.	What family events do we celebrate (birthdays, christenings, weddings etc.)? How do such events make people feel?
2	Choose, make and write celebration cards, e.g. birthday. Read the writing on card to ensure it has the correct message.	Identify numerals on cards and understand what they mean.	Make prizes for party games, pass the parcel and wrap presents.
3	Discuss the order of events of the party. Which games and songs would they like and why? Play with some adult support.	Make dough birthday cakes with different numbers of candles on. Set the table using colour matching tea sets.	Children make birthday cake and other food which can be prepared the day before. Keep it well covered and in the fridge if possible.
4	Open birthday/ celebration cards and read who they are from. Take photo- graphs of the party to record some of the fun.	Play party games and counting the children who are left. Blow out candles.	Get food ready, set the real table and eat the food with good table manners. Everyone helps to tidy up.
5	Children can write down the rules of some party games to make a booklet. See if other children can follow them. Children can play independently in the area making their own celebrations.	Make a pictogram of the children's favourite party game, food, etc.	What other celebrations do families have? Think about children from other faiths and compare their family celebrations using pictures and photographs.

Table 4 Bedroom and bathroom

Date	Role play	House: Bedroom and bathroom	
	Com./lang./lit. development	Mathematical development	Other areas of development
1	Discuss the two areas with the children and decide what props they need. What activities will happen? **Bedroom:** beds, cots, drawers, wardrobe, bedside table, alarm clock. **Bathroom:** bath, shower, toilet, wash basin, soap, toothpaste and brush etc. Think about the roles to be played and the rules that might apply.	Different-sized beds for different sizes of people. Use different sizes of cardboard boxes. Compare the sizes of children's nightclothes, sort into sets using different criteria.	Use catalogues to get ideas to make covers for beds using material and fabric paint. Think about pillows and how they feel. Make other bedroom props.
2	Discuss what happens in the bathroom. Compare bathrooms. Who has showers or baths etc.? Read-bath-time stories and poems (*Wash, Scrub and Brush, Time to Get Out of the Bath Shirley, I Don't Want to Wash My Hands*).	Think about the times when you have a bath and go to bed. What time do they go to bed? Make a class chart. Read '*What's the Time Mr Wolf?*' and play the game.	Use B&Q and other catalogues or visit a showroom to design and make a bath, toilet etc. for the children to pretend to use (use a chair and handle for toilet, boxes for bath and washbasin with decorative taps).
3	Discuss children's bedrooms and compare the items that are in them, games, soft toys, computers, etc. What do the children use their bedroom for?	Look at clocks and count around them. Make observational pictures of clocks and make one for the bedroom. Think about alarm clocks: why do we need them? Set alarms at different times for the children to find. Try some out by recording the alarms and choosing the most effective.	Discuss personal hygiene and sleeping patterns. Importance of sleep for keeping healthy. Sing lullabies.
4	Act out a scenario in a modern bathroom with modern props.	Look how numbers are used to tell people the temperature of water and the air around them. Go around school and	Think about heating and hot water. How are our bedrooms and bathrooms heated today? Compare with

Table 4   *(Contd)*

Date	Role play	House: Bedroom and bathroom	
	Com./lang./lit. development	Mathematical development	Other areas of development
		home and look for numbers referring to temperature.	houses long ago. Think about how much easier it is to stay clean and warm today than it was in past times.
5	Read *Peepo!* How were bathrooms and bedrooms different from those today?	Use capacity as a means of measuring liquid. Experiment with bubble bath and make different quantities of bubbles. Give dolls a bubble bath and record it.	Using *Peepo!* and some new props, recreate a bathroom and bedroom in past times.

Table 5   Chinese New Year

Date	Role play	House: Chinese New Year	
	Com./lang./lit. development	Mathematical development	Other areas of development
1	Read *'Dat's New Year'*. Discuss what happens and the items they will need. Make New Year greeting cards using red and gold. Hang up in house area.	Count and match all the plates and dishes, chopsticks, etc. to see if there are enough for the family. Introduce the wok and other Chinese cooking tools. Look at the shape and the size of them.	Clean and tidy house area and get some fresh flowers to decorate it. Make colourful lanterns and streamers.
2	Make scrolls using Chinese writing in red, gold and black.	Store tools and equipment with silhouettes to help keep the kitchen tidy. Set the table matching items by colour and size.	Decorate the house and begin to make the animal masks.
3	Discuss the type of food that is cooked for the New Year. Look at recipes and try cooking some. Pretend to cook using Chinese techniques. Read and write recipes.	Weigh ingredients using spoonfuls, scales, tools. Measure liquids using a spoon and measuring jug. Use real and pretend ingredients.	Begin to make the dragon's head for the procession. The children experiment with chopsticks and try to pick up food items with them. Read *'Clever Sticks'*

Table 5 *(Contd)*

Date	Role play	House: Chinese New Year	
	Com./lang./lit. development	Mathematical development	Other areas of development
4	Listen to and learn special Chinese songs: 'Gong Ha Fat Choy' song from *Silver Burdett*. Think about lucky cookies and what they would wish for.	Make money bags with decorations on them. Count the coins. Play instruments, carefully beating in a steady rhythm.	The children have a Chinese banquet using chopsticks and special Chinese food that they have made.
5	Discuss what they will need for the procession. Collect items together and do a dragon dance outside the school wearing masks, playing instruments and being led by the dragon.	Discuss the order of the animals in the procession and introduce ordinal numbers.	The children can take photographs and tape the event. They can paint pictures of the procession. Children play independently incorporating all the bits together.

Table 6   Family outing/holiday

Date	Role play	Family outing/holiday	
	Com./lang./lit. development	Mathematical development	Other areas of development
1	Discuss where they are going. What will they need to take? What will they need to get ready?	How many are going? How long for? How long will it take to get there?	Discuss how are they getting there (car, bus, train, aeroplane, boat). Book the tickets. Get the family car ready.
2	Read a day visit account (*Topsy and Tim Visit the Zoo* or any other similar story).	What will they eat? How many of each will we need?	Discuss activities you do at different times of the day. Draw pictures and act out.
3	Write instructions for making sandwiches and other food they need to prepare.	Make shaped food, triangular sandwiches, circular cakes etc.	Design a box or container to carry the different kinds of food in. Flasks, plastic boxes, cool bags etc. Perhaps a packed lunch box.
4	Pretend to go on a trip. Record what happens,	Discuss how far away the venue is. Think	Discuss where you have gone and the activities

Table 6   *(Contd)*

Date	Role play	Family outing/holiday	
	Com./lang./lit. development	Mathematical development	Other areas of development
	e.g. take or pretend to take photographs.	about the distance. Share out the picnic.	and things you will see there.
5	Discuss what happened. Draw pictures and write a simple account with pictures or use a tape recorder so that you can share your outing with your friends.	Sequence the main events of your trip.	Perhaps make a picture map to let the whole class share the experience.

Table 7   Utility room

Date	Role play	House: Utility room	
	Com./lang./lit. development	Mathematical development	Other areas of development
1	Discuss setting up the area as an imaginary utility room. What do they think they will need? Rules that apply when playing. Number of children and roles to be played: mums, dads, children. What household jobs can we do in the area (washing, soaking, spinning, drying clothes, ironing)? Understand the dangers.	Begin to set up area. Decide where equipment can be placed and why. Store tools and equipment with silhouettes to help keep the area tidy. Look at numbers on equipment.	Cut out pictures of machines that help us to wash our clothes (collage). Design and make props, create utility room: washing machines, dryers, wringers, spinners, sinks, lines, irons and boards. Discuss the safety of using certain appliances (electrical).
2	Read *JJ and the Washing Machines* and other books and rhymes related to laundry. Find and read the labels in clothes and discuss the symbols for washing.	Sort clothes using a variety of criteria: size, colour, materials, owner etc.	Look at the different types of materials that clothes are made from and how best to wash them.
3	Read *When Dad Did the Washing*. Develop a situation where a	Weigh ingredients using spoonfuls, scales, tools. Measure liquids using a	Introduce the idea of hygiene and the importance of keeping

19

Table 7   *(Contd)*

Date	Role play	**House:** Utility room	
	Com./lang./lit. development	Mathematical development	Other areas of development
	problem has to be sorted out, e.g. power cut, colours run, clothes shrink or a mechanic has to come out to the home and fix the machine.	spoon and measuring jug.	clothes clean and fresh. Think about a time before machines. Try washing by hand and compare the results and the time taken.
4	Children try to write instructions down for hand and machine washing. They try to recreate the sequence of washing, drying and ironing.	Children use a timer to see which detergent is the quickest. Children give numbered instructions on how to use certain machines. Other children try to follow the instructions.	Think about different types of soaps and powders and how children should never touch them. Look at some stains on clothes and try out different detergents. Record what they discover. Look at the variety of detergent packages and let the children design some.
5	Read *Mrs Mopple's Washing Line*. Discuss how she does her family's washing. Compare to your family wash. Children play independently in area using props correctly.	Time washing by hand and machine.	Look at real tools: old irons, mangles, dolly tubs etc. and try them in play. Draw observational pictures of them. Discuss ironing and general clothes care before we had washing machines.

Table 8   Christmas

Date	Role play	House: Christmas	
	Com./lang./lit. development	Mathematical development	Other areas of development
1	Make Christmas greeting cards for friends and write them.	Count and match plates etc. Make sure there are enough for the family. Introduce some Christmas plates etc. Make an advent calendar and discuss the	Tidy up the house area using vacuum cleaner, brooms and dusters and get it ready for decorating. Get a small Christmas tree.

Table 8 *(Contd)*

Date	Role play	House: Christmas	
	Com./lang./lit. development	Mathematical development	Other areas of development
		numbers and why they are there.	
2	Hang up Christmas cards reading who they are from. Discuss the idea of visiting Santa with a request for a present. Look in catalogues and make lists of what they would like to give to others.	Use the advent calendar looking carefully at all the numbers.	Decorate the tree with shiny shapes and Christmas balls. Add safe battery-operated lights so that the children are able to switch them on and off.
3	Read *The Christmas Story* and other Christmas literature, poems and songs. Play freely in role-play area.	Make Christmas decorations thinking about shapes and patterns.	Pretend to go Christmas shopping in a temporary shop, buying presents for children and adults.
4	Pretend to go round singing carols, visiting other parts of the school. Pretend to have a Christmas party. Think about the items they may need, how one activity is inside and the other traditionally outside.	Predict the amount of paper you will need to wrap and make parcels of special presents the children have pretended to buy.	Encourage the children to realise the joy of Christmas is to be kind, giving and thoughtful to others. Discuss the excitement of giving others surprises.
5	Cook some special Christmas food from real ingredients and dough (Christmas pudding, mince pies). Read and follow simple recipes.	Guess what is inside the presents and open them. Measure ingredients, cook Christmas food and share finished dishes.	Draw observational pictures of the food cooked and of the family Christmas dinner.

Table 9   Moving house

Date	Role play	House: Moving	
	Com./lang./lit. development	Mathematical development	Other areas of development
1	Discuss with the children moving house. Tell the children we are going to move the role-play house. Bring in lots of estate agents' pictures and sheets and read them with the children. Decide which information is important (number of rooms, size, garden, price etc.). Discuss what roles and props we need.	Count and record the number of rooms in own house. Record the colour of the door and the number. Compare each other's houses.	Discuss different kinds of homes (bungalow, flat, terraced, semi-detached/detached houses etc.). Find out and bring information about their own home as if they were ready to sell it.
2	Make a small poster of each child's house and display on wall (photograph or drawing) with a little information about it. Make a class telephone directory so that the estate agent can contact his clients. What will he need in his office? Give the estate agent's and staff names. Begin playing with support.	Think about the cost of your new home. Pay and sign cheques and contracts. Begin to sort the houses into sets (colour, type etc.). Have named labelled keys to match each house picture.	Use polite conversation when playing. Learn the names of the outside parts of the house (roof, walls, chimney, gutters, drain etc.). Find out address and telephone number.
3	The children choose a house. Find out the name of owner, telephone and go and view it. Go back and report orally. Start to buy. Think about contracts and putting children's names on, with the idea of signing their own name.	Book removal van with driver (give name) by telephone, thinking about size and cost. How are you going to pay—with cash, credit card or cheque?	Wrap and pack items from old house. What size of paper or box will you need? If it is a delicate item, what can you use (bubble wrap)? Think about moving big objects to the van. Use a trolley made from a large construction kit.
4	Write labels on items	Pack objects into van,	Use maps to show the

Table 9   *(Contd)*

Date	Role play	House: Moving	
	Com./lang./lit. development	Mathematical development	Other areas of development
	when packed and the room you want them put in. Let the children describe their new home and discuss why it is better. Make Victor's Violet Van (box with wheels but decorated with v v v).	thinking about size and shape. Think about the distance and time taken to travel.	van driver where to go. When the van arrives start to unpack, carefully unwrapping items.
5	Encourage the children to play independently taking on the various roles and carrying through the process of buying, selling and moving house. Use tape recorders to record conversations. Read *Moving Molly*.	Use outside play area and cars to transport items greater distances and the children can count, use stopwatches or egg timers to see how long it takes.	Think about the materials that go to make a house: glass, bricks, metals, wood etc. What properties have they got that make them useful?

HEALTH CARE

Optician's

Play situation

Create an optician's consulting room where eyes can be tested, a waiting room and a fitting room where patients can try on new spectacles. The children can play all the roles of staff and patients to understand the process involved in buying a pair of spectacles. (See Table 10.)

Introductory prompts

Where do we go if we cannot see properly?
Can you go to Boots and just buy any pair of spectacles?
Do you care what your spectacles would look like?
Why do we need to see clearly?
Do you know any other tools that will help you see objects better?

Possible roles

Optician, receptionist, spectacle fitter, patients and cleaners

Resources

Supply your optician's office with costumes, spectacles, mirrors, eye leaflets, sight charts (colour, objects, numerals, shapes and letters), hand lens, binoculars, telescope, special chair, telephone, appointment book, calendar, appointment cards, eye record cards, writing tools, desk and chair for receptionist, magazines and chairs in the waiting area.

See Recommended reading for books about opticians.

Link activities

Make eye pictures using marbling inks.
Collages of eyes from magazines and catalogues.
Make a selection of shaped spectacles.
Recognise and match: shapes, letters, numerals from eye charts.
Talk about looking after your eyes.
Discuss sight as one of the five senses.

Potential learning opportunities

Personal, social and emotional development

The optician's role-play area will help the children to:

Disposition and attitudes

- explore new learning experiences and share knowledge with other children who have had their eyes tested;

Self-confidence and self-esteem

- show that working together as a team can be enjoyable and exciting;

Making relationships/behaviour/self-control

- take turns fairly in the waiting room;
- be polite and say please and thank you;

Self-care

- develop their ability to choose for themselves by selecting their own spectacles;

Sense of community

- take on different character roles to explore for themselves what it is like to work;
- understand that different people have different needs;

Communication, language and literacy

The optician's role-play area will help the children to:

Speaking, listening and communicating

- speak clearly and use appropriate body language to communicate with their peers and adults directly or by telephone;
- ask and answer simple questions from patients about eyes and note personal details;
- encourage them to follow instructions so that roles relate to each other;
- use role play to represent stories relating to sight, e.g. Jesus and the blind man;

Reading

- develop an awareness for environmental print by reading and writing notices and labels for the opticians giving out relevant information;
- match and identify letters, shapes and numbers using eye tests;
- read and share a selection of relevant fiction and non-fiction books about eyes and sight;

Writing

- write names in the appointment book and on spectacle-shaped appointment cards using a wide range of marking tools;
- write times down and pretend to use a clock;
- record what patients can see on the sight charts.

Mathematical development

The optician's role-play area will help the children to:

Matching, sorting and shape

- sort, match and construct spectacles being aware of their colour, size and shape.
- recognise and match shapes, numerals and letters during the eye test;

Representation

- collect and handle data about the colour of children's eyes and record what they find in different ways and styles;

Number

- count reliably the numbers of spectacles and children;
- understand the concept of pairs and begin to count in twos;

Calculations

- understand that spectacles are not free and must be paid for, by putting prices on the spectacles of numerals up to 10p and begin to identify coins and be aware of their value;

Measurement and size

- use standard and non-standard units of measure as a means of sizing spectacles for each individual child: tape measures, rulers and pieces of string;

Time

- understand the idea of times of the day: morning, afternoon and night;
- identify the days of the week;
- understand the importance of having clocks and watches if we are going to get to places on time or early, and not late (appointments).

Knowledge and understanding of the world

The optician's role-play area will help the children to:

Observe and explore/life processes and living things

- observe what their own eyes look like and begin to identify parts of the face;
- understand that everyone's eyes are slightly different;
- understand that the eye is used to see with and we call this sense sight;
- understand that we must look after our eyes;
- experiment with blindfolds and play light and dark games;
- experiment with different lenses and record how they change the ways objects look;
- use torches and investigate how they help us;

Design and make

- design and make resources for the optician's role-play area;
- design and make a pair of spectacles that fit;

ICT

- use My World CD-ROM faces on the computer and make some faces concentrating on the eyes.

Creative development

The optician's role-play area will help the children to:

Exploring media and materials

- make charts, notices and displays for the opticians;
- make spectacles and decorative eyes using a variety of materials and techniques, e.g. marbling eyes;

Music

- learn new rhymes and songs about eyes and perform them;

Imagination

- act as characters in the optician's, creating new characters and original story lines, going and buying new spectacles or not being able to see properly.

Physical development

The optician's role-play area will help the children to:

Movements

- improve fine and gross motor movements and develop hand-eye coordination by using a wide variety of tools and materials;

Health and bodily awareness

- name different parts of the eye and be aware of some of their functions;
- understand the need to keep eyes healthy and how to look after them.

Talking points

In the waiting room and fitting room

Can I have your name please?

Who would you like to see?
When can I come?
How old are you?
What will happen to me?
Will it hurt?
Can you see the shapes, numbers or letters?
Which is the biggest?
Which is the smallest?
What colour spectacles would you like?
Can I try them on?
Do they suit me?
Look in a mirror.
How long will they be?

Key vocabulary

Eyes, sight, eyelashes, eyebrows, pupils, dark, light, optician, patient, spectacles, glasses, magnifying glass, binoculars, microscope, hand lens, making bigger, making smaller, making clearer

Observational focus

Observe the children play and ask them: 'Why do we go to the optician's?' 'What do we need to do when we get there?'

1. Cannot remember any significant information/detail ☐
2. Can remember a small amount of information/detail ☐
3. Can give a full account of how and why you would visit an optician's ☐
4. Can extend their play to create new characters and scenarios ☐

Table 10   Optician's

Date	Role play	Optician's	
	Com./lang./lit. development	Mathematical development	Other areas of development
1	Encourage the children to take on roles. Explain what each character has to do. Explain how and why we make appointments. Encourage question and answer dialogue.	Match colours, shapes, letters and numbers on charts. Identify that the symbols get smaller towards the bottom of the chart.	Parts of the face. Design and make spectacles for themselves.
2	Introduce the	Price spectacles up to	Read leaflets, books and

Table 10 *(Contd)*

Date	Role play	Optician's	
	Com./lang./lit. development	Mathematical development	Other areas of development
	characters needed for the role play and give them identities. Let the children go through the process of making an appointment and having their eyes tested. Choose spectacles.	10p. Count real money and recognise different coins: 1p, 2p, 5p, 10p.	signs and encourage the children to write their own.
3	Use the telephone to take messages. Play independently with minimum adult support. Look at non-fiction books and leaflets about eyes and describe what they look like. Make leaflets about eyes for the waiting room.	How many eyes do we have? How many would two people have?	Encourage children to use My World 'Faces' program on computer and investigate eyes.
4	Devise a system to record what each patient can see. Play independently. Read *Peepo!* and begin to play I Spy.	Record how many symbols the patients can see. Count and group spectacles into sets. Count and predict what one more pair will make.	Play hand-eye coordination games, e.g. threading. Use eyes effectively and safely.
5	Listen to stories about Jesus and the blind man. Explore what it must be like to be blind. Play independently in the optician's.	Count how many objects the patients can identify by using their other senses with blindfolds on.	Play the blindfold game. Discuss how hard life would be if we could not see. What kind of support do blind or partially sighted people have?

Dentist's surgery

Play situation

Create a dental surgery, dental hygienist unit and waiting room where children can experience visiting a dental surgery and begin to understand the importance of looking after their teeth. (See Table 11.)

Introductory prompts

Where do we go if our teeth or mouth hurt?
Has anyone visited a dentist?
What happens there?
Do the treatments hurt?
What do we need to do to keep our teeth healthy?
Where will we buy things to look after our teeth?
How can we set up a dentist's surgery? What will we need?

Possible roles

Dentist, dental nurse, dental hygienist, receptionist and patients

Resources

Supply your dentist's surgery with a dentist's chair, instruments, torch, toothpastes, toothbrushes, dental floss, disclosing tablets, pictures and leaflets about dental care, calendar, clock, writing tools, appointment books, appointment cards, mouth records and a selection of non-fiction books, till and money.
    See Recommended reading for books about dentists.

Link activities

Make a model of the mouth showing other parts: lips, tongue and gums.
Look at the structure of teeth.
Explain that different types of teeth do different jobs.
Our mouths help us to talk. Experiment with tongue tracking. Lean some tongue twisters.
Look at taste as one of the five senses. Try some practical tasting activities.
Collect healthy food.

Potential learning opportunities

Personal, social and emotional development

The dental surgery role-play activities can help the children to:

Disposition and attitudes

- explore a new learning environment and share with other children experiences they may have had at the dentist;

Self-confidence and self-esteem

- develop personal qualities such as imagination, creativity, confidence, humour and persistence while at play;
- be able to express their feelings and understand the feelings of others, e.g. being nervous about visiting the dentist;

Making relationships/behaviour/self-control

- work cooperatively together within certain limits and restrictions of their roles, e.g. patient or dentist, and modify their own actions accordingly;
- take turns and fairly share the equipment and the space;
- recognise and comfort a child who is distressed and unwell in role;

Self-care

- develop an awareness of their own personal needs and be able to select the correct resources for the task, e.g. toothpaste, brushes, mouth washes etc.;
- distinguish being awake and being asleep and role-play going to bed and waking up;
- understand that certain foods are bad for their teeth;

Sense of community

- feel part of a class and share experiences with their peers and supporting adults.

Communication, language and literacy

The dental surgery role-play activities will help children to:

Speaking, listening and communicating

- speak clearly and use appropriate body language to communicate with peers and adults directly, or by telephone, to make appointments or find out personal details or problems of patients;
- ask and answer relevant questions from adults and children about dental care;

Reading

- develop an awareness of reading in the environment by having access to magazines, leaflets, posters, toothpaste tubes etc.;
- read and share a selection of fiction and non-fiction books about the mouth;

Writing

- begin to write down children's personal information in a way they can reread using symbolic writing through to conventional letter forms;

- record the dentist's findings in some form of written record;
- write leaflets and posters about healthy eating and good dental care;
- make a zig-zag book about the sequence of cleaning teeth to display in the waiting room.

Mathematical development

The dental surgery role-play activities will help children to:

Matching, sorting and shape

- match and sort objects considering a variety of criteria, e.g. sorting toothbrushes using two criteria: size and colour;

Number

- record what the dentist can see in picture form: counting teeth;
- use numerals as labels for children's age and dates on dental records;
- count reliably the number of toothbrushes and tubes of toothpaste. Compare their size and colour;

Calculations

- calculate the total of adding two sets of toothbrushes together;

Length, weight, capacity and volume

- explore the ideas of capacity: full, empty, fill, holds more than, holds less than, when using water to clean your teeth or wash your mouth out;

Time

- understand the idea of times of the day: morning, afternoon and night;
- identify the days of the week;
- understand the importance of having watches and clocks if we are going to get to places on time and not be late, e.g. dental appointments.

Knowledge and understanding of the world

The dental surgery role-play activities will help children to:

Observe and explore life processes and living things

- explore their sense of taste and speech to discover new things and discuss observations and investigations they have carried out, e.g. taste testing and sound making;
- understand what they need to keep their mouths healthy;

33

Design and making

- design and make resources for the role-play area: notices, models of mouths and sets of false teeth;

ICT

- use ICT to complement their learning, e.g. Faces (My World CD-ROM), focusing on the mouth;
- use a recording device to record the sounds children can make with their mouths. Tape each child's voice and let the children guess who it is;

Sense of time and place

- have an awareness of the passage of time to make appointments and use days of the week, times of the day and o'clock times;
- understand how our bodies change over a period of time: babies having no teeth, baby teeth coming through, then falling out, new adult teeth growing to replace them;
- follow a routine.

Creative development

The dental surgery role-play activities will help children to:

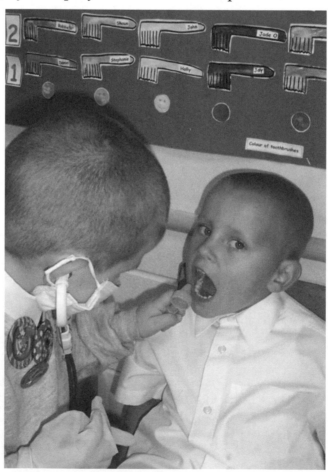

Exploring media and materials

- use a variety of media and tools to create models for the dentist's: mouth, false teeth, dentist, dental nurse etc.;
- make charts, posters and labels giving information about the dentist's for the role-play area;

Music

- listen to and join in songs and rhymes about their bodies, e.g. 'All I Want for Christmas Is My Two Front Teeth', using simple instruments to complement their performance;

Imagination

- use their imagination to recreate what it is like to go to the dentist's;
- let the children create scenarios and try and solve problems, e.g. toothache, appointments double-booked;
- use drama to recount what routines they follow when they go to bed and wake up in the morning.

Physical development

The dental surgery role-play activities will help children to:

Movements

- use a wide range of tools and materials to develop coordination by handling the dentist's tools and mark-making equipment improving fine and gross motor control;

Health and bodily awareness

- name parts of the body related to the mouth and understand some of their functions;
- recognise the need for personal hygiene and good diet to keep healthy.

Talking points

What is your name, age and address?
What is wrong with you?
Where does it hurt?
What will happen to me?
When can I come?
How do I keep my teeth clean?
How much will it cost?
How many patients have you seen?
Can you fit one more patient in?

Key vocabulary

Surgery, dentist, toothbrush, toothpaste, injection, drill, filling, extraction, gas, sleep, toothache, please, thank you

Observational focus

Ask the children what happens at the dentist. How can we keep our teeth healthy?

1. Cannot remember any significant information/detail ☐
2. Can remember a small amount of information and detail ☐
3. Can give a full account of how to visit a dentist's, what happens there and how to care for their teeth ☐
4. Can extend their play and create new characters and scenarios ☐

Table 11   Dentist's surgery

Date	Role play	Health: Dentist's surgery	
	Com./lang./lit. development	Mathematical development	Other areas of development
1	Discuss what goes on at the dentist's. Read *Topsy and Tim Go to the Dentist* or a similar story. Start to put up signs and posters and discuss what they say. Add magazines and leaflets so the patients can read while they are waiting.	Discuss the children's ages. Look at the telephone and begin to recognise the numerals. Make up telephone numbers for each child and for the dental surgery. Use the telephone in between classrooms dialing the correct three digits.	Set up role-play area with the children and decide what is needed. What will we have to make? Discuss who has been to the dentist and what happens there. Check-ups, fillings, extractions. (Usborne First Experiences, *Going to the Dentist*.) Start to make a dentist college and give him/her an identity.
2	Act out visiting the dentist, allowing the children to select different roles. Discuss each role. Start making an appointment book and record cards with teeth on. Discuss what personal details need to be written on them. Learn some rhymes relating to teeth.	Record what the dentist can see. How many teeth need to come out? How many fillings do they need? Discuss queries and the order people enter the surgery: first, second etc.	Look at the parts of the mouth. Notice that all the children's teeth are different. Discuss the jobs teeth do. Make a large model mouth and some false teeth.

Table 11 *(Contd)*

Date	Role play	Health: Dentist's surgery	
	Com./lang./lit. development	Mathematical development	Other areas of development
3	Start making health care posters and leaflets. Read some non-fiction books about teeth and dental care. Let the children play and at the end gather up all the writing the children have done and encourage them to read it back to the group.	Sort and group toothbrushes. Use colour and size as criteria. Record the colour of all the children's toothbrushes and display them.	Start to look at how the children can look after their teeth. Think about the routine of care. Think about which kinds of food are good for your teeth and which may cause harm. Taste some food (salty, sour, sweet).
4	Make a zig-zag book sequencing how we clean our teeth for display. Introduce a dental hygienist to the role play and discuss her job.	Measure the capacity of glasses of water and mouthwash used when cleaning teeth. Use mathematical language: full, empty, half full, fill, holds more, holds less. Think about syringes and the amount of water they can hold.	Look at the routine of going to sleep. Act it out focusing on dental hygiene. Introduce words relating to the passage of time: earlier, later, night, morning, afternoon etc. Relate them to opening and closing time and appointment times so everyone does not come at once.
5	Look at environmental print in the role play area. Why do people use it? Look at packets and bottles related to dental care. Read *Bangers and Mash Toothday* and other stories.	Collect data about children's favourite toothpaste. Discuss how it can be displayed.	Introduce ICT: My World CD-Rom program 'Faces' where the children can build up faces and look at different types of teeth and mouths and print them off.

Doctor's surgery, baby clinic and hospital

Play situation

Create a doctor's surgery and waiting room with additional clinics such as the baby clinic and a chemist's shop. The children will play the roles of staff and patients and some dolls will be included as the babies. The children will begin to understand why they go to the doctor's and how to go about making appointments. This is then extended to involve a hospital for more serious cases and an ambulance service to get the patients there. The children identify some of the main areas in a hospital and take on some of the roles of the workers. (See Tables 12–14.)

Introductory prompts

Where do we go if we do not feel well?
What do we think the doctor will do?
Do any other people work at the doctor's?
Why do we need to make an appointment?
Can anyone else help us if we feel ill?
What happens in the chemist's shop?
Why do babies need to go to a clinic?
What happens if the doctor is unable to treat you?
How do we get to hospital?
Who works in a hospital?
Why do you sometimes need to stay in?
Has anyone had an operation?
Has anyone ever had an X-ray?

Possible roles

Doctors, nurses, health visitor, chemist, receptionists, patients and babies (dolls), radiographers, surgeons

Resources

Furnish your doctor's room and waiting room with chairs, posters, magazines, appointments book, body cards, clock, calendar, writing tools, record cards, doctor's tools, table and surgery, torches, bottles, spoons, tins and prescription pads, bandages and plasters, cots, scales, operating theatre, x-ray machine and x-rays.

See Recommended reading for books about doctors and hospitals.

Link activities

Make collages of doctors and nurses and give them identities.
Make bodies and identify the various parts and discuss what some of them do.
Look at hand and footprints and be creative and mathematical.
Discuss children's experiences of visiting the doctor's and hospitals.
Think about what makes us healthy, food, exercise and being happy.
Collect a selection of healthy food and chat about it.

Potential learning opportunities

Personal, social and emotional development

The health care activities in the role-play area will help the children to:

Disposition and attitude

- explore new learning environments and relate them to their personal experiences of visiting medical centres and hospitals;
- develop personal qualities such as imagination, creativity, confidence, humour and persistence;

Self-confidence and self-esteem

- be able to express their feelings and to understand the feelings of others, e.g. a child being nervous about visiting the doctor;

Making relationships, behaviour and self-control

- work cooperatively together within certain limits and restrictions of their roles. To take turns and share fairly space and resources;
- develop a caring attitude towards others. Modify their own actions accordingly and show consideration to others, e.g. a nurse in role to recognise and comfort a child who is distressed or ill;

Self-care

- develop an awareness of their own personal needs and be able to select the correct doctor's tools, writing equipment and materials;
- develop an awareness of their own personal needs and take off and put on clothes with increasing independence, e.g. uniforms;

Sense of community

- understand that health workers are an important part of the local community and be aware of some of the local buildings they use, e.g. health centres and dentist's.

Communication, language and literacy

The health care activities in the role-play area will help the children to:

Speaking, listening and communicating

- speak clearly and use appropriate body language to communicate with peers and adults directly or by telephone;

39

- ask and answer relevant questions from adults and children about health and personal details about patients;

Reading and linking sounds to letters

- read and share fiction books, stories, rhymes and poems, non-fiction books and magazines, leaflets, posters and environmental print about the body and health;
- read back information they have written about the patients;

Writing

- write down children's personal information in a way they can reread using symbolic writing through to conventional letter forms;
- develop ways of recording doctor's findings in some form of written record (body shaped card);
- write leaflets and posters about healthy living and exercise, how to keep your heart healthy.

Mathematical development

The health care activities in the role-play area will help the children to:

Matching and sorting shapes

- match shapes of doctor's tools and always return to the correct picture;
- sort out patients using simple criteria (hair colour, illness, eye colour);
- match dolls to armbands or beds in the hospital.

Matching and ordering

- order patients, dolls from the tallest to the shortest;

Representation

- record what the doctor can see in picture form;

Number

- use numerals as labels for the children's age;
- count the dolls present and order them, e.g. waiting for an operation;
- count reliably the number of body parts, e.g. arms, hands, toes and fingers. Then count them on different numbers of children. Develop the skills of counting in 2s and 5s;

Calculations

- begin simple practical addition and subtraction operations using up to five dolls, tablets, beds, pillows etc;

Measuring capacity, volume, weight and length

- investigate small volumes by using small units of measurement, e.g. spoonfuls, so they begin to explore capacity;
- understand that you can weigh objects to see how heavy they are, e.g. dolls at the baby clinic;

Time

- understand the idea of times of the day: morning, afternoon and night;
- identify the days of the week and use them to make appointments;
- understand the importance of having watches and clocks if we are going to get to places on time and not be late.

Knowledge and understanding of the world

The health care activities in the role-play area will help the children to:

Observe and explore

- use their sense of touch to discover new things;
- discuss observations and investigations they have carried out, e.g. hand and foot printing;

Life processes

- have some knowledge of the organs inside their bodies (brain, heart, lungs, digestive tract and the skeleton) and their function;
- understand what they need to keep healthy;
- design and make resources for the role-play area: notices, models of bodies and observe how they change with growth due to the passage of time; zig-zag books showing babies to adults; baby pictures: guess who this was;
- use ICT to complement their learning, e.g. CD-ROM The Doctor's Surgery (Granada).

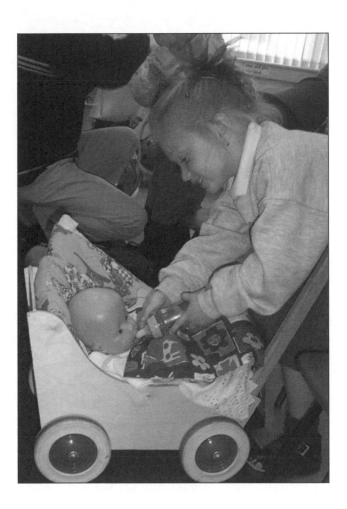

Creative development

The health care activities in the role-play area will help the children to:

- use a variety of media and tools to create collages of doctors, nurses and hospital staff (e.g. radiographers);
- use the skills involved in printing to create personal body part pictures for each child's hand or foot using lots of different materials and media including plaster of Paris;

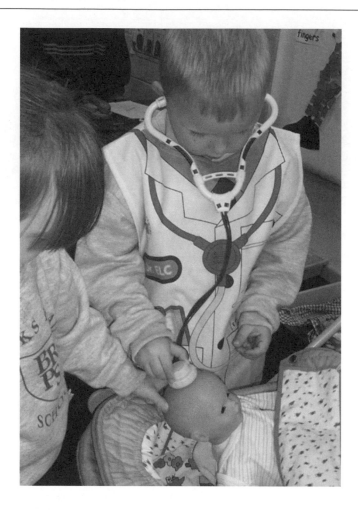

- listen to and join in with songs and rhymes about their bodies;
- use simple instruments to complement their performance;
- use their imagination to recreate what it is like to go to the doctor's and hospital and begin to create new scenarios.

Physical development

The health care activities in the role-play area will help the children to:

- use a wide range of doctor's tools, mark-making tools, other equipment and materials to develop coordination;
- name parts of the body and begin to understand their functions.
- recognise the need for personal hygiene and good diet to keep healthy.

Talking points

What is your name, address and age?
How do you feel?
Who would you like to see?

What time/day would you like to come?
Why does the doctor examine you?
Why do babies go to clinics?
What does your baby weigh?
Who is the heaviest?
What food does your baby eat?
Where do we go to get our medicines?
What will happen to me?
When can I come?
How many patients have you seen?
Can you fit one more patient in?
Have you ever been to hospital?
What do you think your bones are for?
What happens if you break one?
Have you ever had an operation?

Key vocabulary

Medical staff, beds, stethoscope, tablets, medicines, spoons, injections, care, gentle, scales, weight, child, baby, man, lady, teenager, body parts, clean, hygiene, sterile, office, computer, telephone, writing tools and materials, diaries, appointment books, body shaped record cards

Observational focus

Ask the children what happens at the doctor's/baby clinic/hospital. How can we keep our bodies healthy?

1. Cannot remember any significant information/detail ☐
2. Can remember a small amount of information and detail ☐
3. Can give a full account of how to see a doctor or visit a hospital ☐
4. Can extend play by creating new characters and scenarios ☐

Table 12   Doctor's surgery

Date	Role play	Health: Doctor's surgery	
	Com./lang./lit. development	Mathematical development	Other areas of development
1	What do you go to the doctor's for? Introduce the new vocabulary. Share stories and experiences about going to the doctor's surgery. Introduce the	Match doctor's tools to a mat with silhouettes to find where they go. Count the number of hands, feet, fingers, eyes, etc. Count in twos.	Set up role-play area with all the areas you need for a doctor's surgery: waiting room, surgery, reception, pharmacy. Make some of the props, e.g. beds,

Table 12 *(Contd)*

Date	Role play	Health: Doctor's surgery	
	Com./lang./lit. development	Mathematical development	Other areas of development
	roles, costumes and equipment that the children will use and wear.		files, doctor's table.
2	Introduce the telephone and appointment book for the receptionist.	Write telephone numbers down and pretend to ring them. Use a public telephone box. How are they different from telephoning from home?	Make large body sized pictures to name different parts of the body.
3	Introduce body shaped cards for the children to write down patients' names and what the doctors and nurses discover about them and colour in the body part where there is a problem.	Count patients in the waiting room. Discuss who is first, second etc. Use bandages and dressings of different sizes, shapes and materials to treat the patients.	Make large collages of nurses and doctors and give them identities.
4	Introduce the idea of writing a prescription and taking it to the pharmacy.	Encourage the pharmacy to give prescriptions for tablets and medicine. Write instructions on sticky labels which are attached to the bottles and jars, e.g. 1, 2, 3, a day.	Discuss the importance of hands and the sense of touch for doctors and nurses. Play touch games. Emphasise the dangers of playing with real tablets and medicines.
5	Read non-fiction books about medical jobs. Encourage the children to play independently in the area.	Use spoons of different sizes to measure capacity while giving patients medicine. Count tablets and give to dolls as the label states.	Introduce the children to ICT, At the Doctor's, where they can explore the surgery, use special doctor's tools, count tablets, give injections and medicine and write prescriptions which can be printed out with the patient's name on.

Table 13   Hospital ward and operating theatre

Date	Role play	Health: Hospital ward and operating theatre	
	Com./lang./lit. development	Mathematical development	Other areas of development
1	Discuss why we go to hospital. Has anyone ever visited or had to stay in hospital? Read *Topsy and Tim Go to Hospital* or any similar book. Begin to ask the children what jobs there are in a hospital and what materials they will need to set it up.	Discuss the number of people who visit or stay in hospital and how each one has a number label. Give the dolls labels as they come to hospital.	Use different sized boxes to make beds for dolls.
2	Look at non-fiction books about the body. Give each doll a record card (colour, names or numbers to match the doll's bed) with a name to record what happens to them and what medication they may need.	Match the dolls to the different coloured beds. Each bed has a matching record card. On these cards write the doll's special hospital number and name. Count the dolls and match with cups, bottles, trays, books etc.	Think about what is inside our bodies: bones and organs. Investigate by looking at X-rays, skeletons and pictures of different organs: brain, heart, stomach etc. Make bone pictures to use as X-rays. Make an X-ray machine.
3	Use telephones to communicate between the different departments (intercoms). Discuss what they may need to say to each other. Look at non-fiction books about the jobs people do in hospitals.	Discuss how to get an ambulance if you need one. Use a telephone and dial 999. Think about the other emergency services.	With wheeled toys go to and from the role-play hospital. Discuss directions. Think about what is inside the ambulance. Make large pictures.
4	Imagine what it would be like staying in hospital. Draw pictures and discuss. Write about how you may feel and the items you would need. Have child-sized bed in the hospital for the children to be patients too.	Count forwards and backwards to make the children sleep during their pretend operation.	Discuss the idea of having an operation and the hospital staff who may be involved. Design a wheeled trolley to transport patients (dolls) around the hospital.

Table 13 *(Contd)*

Date	Role play	Health: Hospital ward and operating theatre	
	Com./lang./lit. development	Mathematical development	Other areas of development
5	When people are ill they receive get well cards and gifts to cheer them up. Children could make some for various patients. Play independently in the hospital, writing and recording what happens.	Continue to recognise and write numerals around the hospital. Look at clocks and name different parts of the day: morning, afternoon, evening, night.	Discuss the idea of people working shifts. People need to be in the hospital day and night. Do any parents work shifts and how does it affect them?

Table 14 Baby clinic

Date	Role play	Health: Baby clinic	
	Com./lang./lit. development	Mathematical development	Other areas of development
1	Discuss what happens when a baby goes to the clinic. Why do they need to go? Discuss who works there and the equipment they use. Have non-fiction books and catalogues. Discuss what they will need to set up a baby clinic.	Set up weighing and measuring equipment. Use school scales and encourage the children to make their own balance.	Find pictures of babies from catalogues and make a montage. Children bring in photographs of themselves and family members as babies.
2	Introduce record cards with babies' name, address, age and weight recorded on them. Children try to record the information.	Encourage the children to use the correct comparative language for weight: heavy, light, heavier, lighter and the same. Use scales independently looking at what happens to them. Record the weights and size by writing numbers on the babies' record card.	Find pictures of children of different ages and try to sequence them.
3	Read Early Learning Centre catalogues for group reading and begin to write orders	Put baby dolls in order of weight. Record weights and write down numbers.	Discuss what helps babies to grow healthy and strong (correct feeding and care). Make

Table 14   *(Contd)*

Date	Role play	Health: Baby clinic	
	Com./lang./lit. development	Mathematical development	Other areas of development
	for family members and friends.		up baby bottles and feed the dolls.
4	Make zig-zag books to illustrate the changes in babies and children as they grow.	Measure the height of the dolls and themselves using a height chart. Use logic people and try to sort into three sizes. Use correct mathematical language: big, little, large, small, bigger, smaller etc.	Use photographs to make observational drawing and paintings to decorate the clinic.
5	Discuss how the games and toys children play with change as they grow. What toys do their brothers and sisters play with? Go to different classrooms and compare the toys the children play with and the activities they do.	Compare their heights and weights to the dolls. Record findings.	Make a Guess Who display with the photographs by taking current photographs of the children and playing matching games using baby photographs.

SHOPS AND SERVICES

Sports centre

Play situation

Create an area where children can exercise and explore how their own body works, moves and stretches, just like the gym where their mum, dad and friends might go. Introduce new games and equipment, for example: weights, steps and exercise tapes for the children to use independently. (See Table 15.)

Introductory prompts

Where do we go if we want to exercise?
What do you think you do there?
Do any children belong to clubs or visit sports centres?
How do you use a sports centre and how much does it cost?
Why do we enjoy playing active games?
How do they make us feel? Why?
Is it important to look after our bodies?
How do we do it?

Possible roles

Fitness instructors, clients, receptionist, cleaners, sports staff

Resources

Provide your sports centre with a cash desk, money, tickets, writing tools, paper, card, posters, PE equipment, steps, weights, stop-watch, race track, sports clothes, footwear, shower, identity cards with photographs on.
  See Recommended reading for books about sports.

Link activities

Make collages and paintings of children exercising.
Look at footprints and be creative and mathematical.
Make shoe and print matches. Discuss functions of different kinds of footwear.
Discuss children's experiences of visiting clubs and sports centres.
Think about what makes us healthy: food, exercise and contentment.
Collect a selection of healthy food and chat about it.

Potential learning opportunities

Personal, social and emotional development

The sports centre role-play area helps the children to:

Disposition and attitude

- explore a new learning environment and share previous personal experiences with others about visiting a sports centre;
- work cooperatively together in pairs and small groups within certain limits and restrictions of their roles;

Self-confidence and self-esteem

- develop personal qualities such as confidence and persistence by improving their skills in a chosen task, e.g. catching a ball; or be willing to tackle new challenges;
- be aware of their own personal needs and be able to select the correct resources for the task e.g. ball for football;

Making relationships/behaviour/self-control

- take turns and share fairly space and play resources in the sports centre;
- explore the idea of rules for games with sports equipment;
- develop a sense of pride in their own achievements as they tackle new challenges;
- recognise and respect differences and similarities between themselves and others and appreciate that their friends are good at a variety of different skills;

Self-care

- take care of their own personal needs and take off and put on clothes with increasing independence;

Sense of community

- be aware of others in the local or worldwide community who need help and support and organise, with adult support, a sponsored event (sponsored jogathon or walk).

51

Communication, language and literacy

The sports centre role-play area helps the children to:

Speaking, listening and communicating

- speak clearly using appropriate body language to communicate directly or by telephone and other equipment to ask and answer clients' questions and requests;
- follow instructions for movements and new activities;
- tell the group about what they have achieved, e.g. learning how to skip, catch a ball etc.;
- develop ways of recording which child is doing which activity;

Reading and linking sounds to letters

- read and share a selection of movement books e.g. *We're Going on a Bear Hunt*, *Toddlerobics*;
- use role play to retell the stories using photographs to help and discuss the final production, perhaps to be shown in front of an audience;
- develop an awareness of reading using the environmental print and by reading magazines, leaflets, posters and non-fiction books about the body and keeping fit;

Writing

- develop confidence and enjoyment of writing using the writing table and role-play area to complement their play. Write names in the appointment book and on action-shaped cards. Make sports centre identification cards with children's names and photographs on for them to use freely;
- make books about what they can do;
- write leaflets and posters about healthy living and exercise and how to keep your heart healthy.

Mathematical development

The sports centre role-play area helps the children to:

Number

- count reliably a number of objects or activities, e.g. number of hops or jumps, and record the results, collect the data and display it in a variety of ways (pictograms, recording tapes, photographs, tally cards);
- have races and discuss ordinal numbers (first, second), and begin to predict and record who comes first, second. . .;

Time

- identify the days of the week and different times of the day, e.g. morning, evening;

- understand the importance of having watches and clocks if we are going to get to places on time and not be late;

Length

- measure the tracks for activities in non-standard units of measurement;

Weight

- measure the weight of objects using non-standard measurements and put objects in order of weight (weight-lifting equipment).

Knowledge and understanding of the world

The sports centre role-play area helps the children to:

Observe and explore

- use their senses to observe how their body felt after exercise;
- discuss observations and investigations they have carried out, e.g. foot printing;

Life processes and living things

- understand and name basic body parts and skeleton and have a knowledge of some of the internal organs and their functions;

Design and making

- make containers for easy access of equipment with clear labels on display;

ICT

- use a digital camera to record their friends' achievements;

Sense of time

- have an awareness of the passage of time.

Creative development

The sports centre role-play area helps the children to:

Exploring media and materials/making

- use a variety of media and tools to create a collage of sports activities;
- use the skills involved in printing to create personal body part pictures for each child using lots of different materials and media including plaster of Paris, papier mâché, wire, wood etc.;

Music

- listen to and join in songs and rhymes about their bodies, e.g. 'Everybody do this', 'I've got a body';
- use simple instruments to complement their performance;

Imagination

- use role play and drama to recreate stories using movements, e.g. *Toddlerobics*, using photographs and their own stories and ideas.

Physical development

The sports centre role-play area helps the children to:

Movement

- improve fine and gross motor movements by experimenting with different sports equipment and clothing;
- experiment with different ways of moving: walking, running, jumping, hopping, skipping, sliding, shuffling, rolling and crawling;
- develop an awareness of speed, shape, direction and level of movements;
- follow the instructions to start and stop while playing simple group and class games;
- jump off objects, e.g. boxes;
- start to take their body weight on different parts of their bodies;
- use wheeled toys to move about with;
- make a sequence of three movements and join them together;

Sense of space

- develop a sense of space so that they can move uninhibitedly;

Using equipment

- play simple games with rules, e.g skittles;
- develop hand-eye coordination using balls and play equipment;
- use a variety of writing tools to record events;

Use tools and materials

- use a wide range of tools and materials to develop coordination (competitions: who can put in the most pegs?);
- use a variety of small equipment to improve fine motor skills, e.g. puzzles and beads;

Health and bodily awareness

- name parts of the body related to the mouth and understand some of their functions;

- encourage sustained physical activity and investigate what it does to their bodies;
- recognise the need for personal hygiene daily and after exercise and good diet to keep healthy.

Talking points

What activity would you like to do?
Have you ever done it before?
What equipment do you need?
How many are there?
What time would you like to come?
How much does it cost?
What happens to your heart when you run?
What kind of food is healthy?
What effect does smoking have on people?

Key vocabulary

Fit, exercise, balls, mats, parachute, frisbees, bean bags, throwing, kicking, catching, movements, sequence, heart, beats, bikes, races, count, record, time

Observational focus

Observe and ask the children what happens at the sports centre. How can they keep their bodies healthy?

1. Cannot remember any significant information/detail ☐
2. Can remember a small amount of information and detail ☐
3. Can give a full account of how to go to a sports centre and how to keep their bodies healthy ☐
4. Can extend play and create new characters and scenarios ☐

Table 15   Sports centre

Date	Role play	Sports centre	
	Com./lang./lit. development	Mathematical development	Other areas of development
1	Talk to the children about their hobbies and where they go to do them. Who works at the sports centre and what equipment do they use? Arrange a visit to the local one. Children draw pictures of themselves doing sports.	Make tickets and discuss the cost of doing different activities.	Collect some equipment with the children to set up a sports centre, name it and make signs. Discuss children's personal photographs, badges and certificates. Take photographs and make membership cards.
2	Introduce the characters needed for the role play and give them identities. Let the children go through the process of buying tickets and doing activities. Discuss the different clothes you wear for different things (changing room).	Count real money and recognise different coins: 1p, 2p, 5p, 10p, 50p and one pound coin. Ensure each child has a ticket. Introduce changing baskets for changing into kit with tickets.	Read leaflets, books and signs and encourage the children to write their own. Read *Toddlerobics* and act out using all the actions and taking photographs.
3	Use the telephone to take messages, ask and answer questions about times and activities. Look at simple timetables and design one for the class sports centre. Play independently.	Count activities, e.g. the number of jumps in a set time. Use stopwatches and egg timers to measure the time.	Investigate what happens to your body when you exercise. Listen to your heart. Discuss briefly how the heart operates.

Table 15 *(Contd)*

Date	Role play	Sports centre	
	Com./lang./lit. development	Mathematical development	Other areas of development
4	Watch a sports broadcast and listen to the commentator. Encourage the children to play at being commentators while other children are performing. Read *Sports Day*. Play independently.	Have races on the outside track and record first, second and third. Let the children make badges and certificates. Make sure every child wins something.	Plan a fund raising event for the class involving exercise.
5	Bring in a selection of newspaper accounts and read them to the children. Use the children's photographs and write about the event as if it were in the newspaper. Children play independently in the sports centre.		

Greengrocer's

Play situation

Create a shop where people can go and buy fresh fruit and vegetables. Gradually introduce other food types and different types of packaging and storage. The shop comprises a trolley park, baskets, shelves with food displayed, scales, till, packers and bag carrying service, and car park. People are able to drive there in cars, walk there or take the bus. They will be able to choose what food they would like to buy, purchase it, pay for it and take it home. (See Table 16.)

Introductory prompts

Where can I go to buy food?
What sort of food would you need to buy?
Do your mum and dad ever go to the greengrocer's or the supermarket?
What else can you buy at the greengrocers' and supermarket?
Why do we need to buy food?
Are all greengrocers' and supermarkets the same?
What happens when you go there?
How could we set up a greengrocer's in the role-play area?
What will we need?

Possible roles

Shop assistants, managers, cashier, customers, shelf-stackers, delivery van drivers, cleaners

Resources

Supply your greengrocer's shop with costumes, trolleys and baskets, leaflets, money, tills, scales, uniforms, shelves, pretend and real food, bags and boxes for packing, mark-making tools and paper for making signs, labels and shopping lists, telephones and computers for online shopping.

See Recommended reading for books about greengrocers and their produce.

Link activities

Deal with coins, money and prices of goods for sale.
Write for different purposes: shopping lists, orders, labels, advertisements and displays.
Wrap and pack food using appropriate amounts and types of materials.
Sort food into sets using different criteria.
Cook and taste different kinds of fruit and vegetables.
Record how the fruit and vegetables change when cooked.

Potential learning opportunities

Personal, social and emotional development

The greengrocer's shop can help children to:

Attitudes

- explore new learning experiences and share with other children who have been to a greengrocer's with their parents;

Self-confidence and self-esteem

- improve their confidence and begin to develop their own personal character and personality;
- play and show excitement while working together as a team;
- take on different character roles to explore for themselves a place of work (shopper, cashier, shelf-stacker etc.);

Making relationships/behaviour/self-control

- wait patiently in a queue and take their turn, and remember to be polite and say please and thank you to one another;

- choose for themselves and select their own baskets, trolleys or fruit and vegetables;
- be cooperative and work together considering the needs and feelings of those around them;

Self-care

- play and work independently in the role-play greengrocer's shop;
- feel confident to ask for help and advice from the shop workers and adults supporting their play;

Sense of community

- develop a sense of belonging to a community within their class and the wider outside community (visit to supermarket and greengrocer's).

Mathematical development

The greengrocer's shop can help children to:

Matching and sorting

- match and sort 2-D and 3-D shapes: fruit, vegetables and packages;
- put food in the shop into appropriately labelled shelves and boxes;
- recognise and match numerals and letters on labels and shopping lists;
- sort and match different coins and notes looking at the pictures and writing on each one;

Number

- count reliably up to ten objects and begin to recognise numerals in the environment (prices and quantities);
- be familiar with and begin to use language such as more than, less than, same, when dealing with money etc.;
- find the total number of objects combining two sets of fruit and vegetables, e.g. a bag of apples and a bunch of bananas;
- understand and use money, and handle it in a play situation;
- name most common coins and begin to understand that each coin has a different value;
- exchange coins for the same value and give change in cash transactions;
- understand that items are not free and must be paid for by putting prices on the objects to be bought of numerals up to 10p;
- discuss the position of the fruit and vegetables in the shop using the correct positional language;

Measuring/size/area/weight/length/capacity

- have an awareness of the size of objects and how this will affect packing them;

- compare the weights of different food packages and put in order of weight using appropriate vocabulary;

Time

- have an awareness of times of the day, shop opening hours and staff working hours;
- order the days of the week in the correct sequence.

Communication, language and literacy

The greengrocer's shop can help children to:

Speaking, listening and communicating

- speak clearly and use appropriate body language to communicate to get attention, to defend their own interests and to be understood by friends and adults;
- name fruit and vegetables and describe what each looks like and how it tastes by playing guessing games;
- develop questioning techniques using how, when, why and where, about the produce and other shop matters;
- give, understand and act upon complex instructions ('put the little green apple on the top shelf next to the large oranges');
- respond to and use appropriate social conventions such as please and thank you when dealing with people;

Reading

- read back shopping lists they have written to the greengrocer;
- recognise words connected to the topic (apples, bananas, carrots, bargain, sale, open, closed);
- understand the need to read and begin to predict what the print might say (read environmental print, notices and labels, information leaflets and advertisements);

Writing

- understand the need to be able to write;
- write names on order forms using a variety of mark-making tools and materials, be able to use emergent writing and develop through symbols to correct letter formations;
- understand and use writing to communicate with others, e.g. send orders, shopping lists, price lists, notes, record information and be able to inform others of it;
- use drama to represent stories relating to the shops: *The Shopping List*, *Oliver's Stories* and *Stone Soup*.

Knowledge and understanding of the world

The greengrocer's shop can help children to:

Observing, exploring and classifying

- observe and investigate the products on sale in the shop;
- use their senses and aids (lens) to help sort and classify fruits and vegetables according to observable attributes and taste;

Materials and their properties

- cook, observe and record changes when food is cooked or cooled (appearance and taste);

Life processes and living things

- understand that fruit and vegetables are grown on plants and try growing food from seeds;
- name some different kinds of fresh food;
- develop an awareness of the similarities and differences between foods and describe what they see;

Design and making

- develop a curiosity and interest in their local environment: visit the local shops;

- explore writing tools and their uses in the work place;
- design and construct models for use in the shop: the strongest box;

ICT

- record conversations in the shop and share experiences with their peers later.
- use a computer program from My World to improve mouse control and coordination by sorting fruit and make printouts;
- use cooking appliances and tools confidently to cook fruit and vegetables;

A sense of place

- show some awareness of their local surroundings by visiting shops.

Creative development

The greengrocer's shop can help children to:

Exploring media and materials

- use creative materials to construct and develop the role-play area;
- make collages, observation work and print pictures to decorate the role-play shop;
- look at great artists (still lifes by Cezanne and Jun Kishimoto) and use them to inspire the children to create pictures to decorate the shop;

Music

- sing songs and rhymes connected to shopping, food and cooking: *Tom Thumb's Musical Maths*: 'Cherries on a plate', 'One Banana', 'Supermarket shop', Apusskidu: 'Bananas in Pyjamas';

Imagination

- act in role as characters in the greengrocer's shop to show how the shop operates;
- copy and extend stories they have heard about food and act them out;
- create their own stories using the props available or making new ones

Physical development

The greengrocer's shop can help children to:

Movement

- improve fine and gross motor movements by handling food, money and packaging materials;

Sense of space

- explore moving heavy loads in wheeled toys (trolley) and carrying them in bags and boxes being aware of safety issues;

Using tools and materials

- gain increasing control of clothes and fastenings while dressing up;
- develop hand-eye coordination by using a variety of tools and materials: tools to prepare food with.

Key vocabulary

food, colours, textures, shelves, trolley, basket, size, cheques, large, small, inside, under, over, up, down, next to, choose, collect, cost, money, till, shopping list, please, thank you

Talking points

What do I need to buy food?
Where can we find what we want?
What are you going to choose?
How much do we need?
How much will it cost?
Can you remember what you have bought?
How much change have you got?
Where do you keep your money?
Did you find everything you needed?

Observational focus

Observe and ask the children: 'Why do we go to the greengrocer's?' 'What do we need to do?'

1. Cannot remember any significant information/detail ☐
2. Can remember a small amount of information/detail ☐
3. Can give a full account of how and why you would visit a greengrocer's ☐
4. Can extend play by creating new characters and scenarios ☐

Table 16 Greengrocer's

Date	Role play	Shops: Greengrocer's	
	Com./lang./lit. development	Mathematical development	Other areas of development
1	Discuss going to the shops to buy food. Has anyone visited a greengrocer's or supermarket? Share ideas and discuss what they sell. Read *Oliver's Fruit Salad* and other books relating to fresh food. Discuss what they will need to set up shop.	Look at the fruit and vegetables and match to outlines. Make sets of foods that have similarities. Look at the shape and the size of them.	Become familiar with the names of foods and what they look like. Taste some foods and record whether they do or do not like them. Record and observe what the fruits and vegetables look like when cut (Kishimoto pictures).
2	Write labels and adverts for products. Use pictures and words. Introduce the idea of writing shopping lists beginning with pictures, emergent writing and moving onto matching words.	Begin to set up the shop. Discuss the shelving, where the food will be placed and why. How many items are to be packed into each package? Write/draw the number of items you want on a shopping list.	Look at non-fiction books and discover information about fresh foods. Cut out pictures of foods to decorate the shop. Think about how food is packaged: fresh, frozen, tinned and dried, to help keep it fresh. Introduce the idea of the importance of hygiene when handling food.
3	Let the children choose their roles and begin to develop play in the shop. Let them develop scenarios and begin to understand what happens when you are inside a shop with adult support.	Introduce money and price the goods for sale. Make price tags with coins on (1p coin, 2p coin etc.). Try calculating the totals.	Read *Handa's Surprise* to the children and encourage them to find new fruits and taste them. Act out the story.
4	Encourage the children to play independently in the shop. Set the children a problem to solve, e.g. a customer that bought some rotten fruit...... What can be done?	Let the children make price tags for goods either drawing, rubbing coins or writing the prices on.	The children can do observational work showing the produce.

Table 16   *(Contd)*

Date	Role play	Shops: Greengrocer's	
	Com./lang./lit. development	Mathematical development	Other areas of development
5	Read *S tone Soup* and *Oliver's Vegetables*. Record recipes and sequence the instructions.	Use real fruit/ vegetables in the shop and towards the end of the session make a fruit salad or vegetable soup, counting them, for the children to share.	The children can take photographs and tape instructions for making fruit salad or soup. They can paint pictures of themselves using different tools (knives, spoons, forks etc.).

Post office

Play situation

Create a post office and shop where the children can go to buy stamps and materials for writing letters, posting parcels, saving money, paying bills and collecting forms for car tax, passports and driving licences. It comprises a counter, form and information desk, postbox, scales, stand which sells pens and stationery, and car park. People are able to drive there in cars, park, walk there or take the bus. They will be able to choose, write, wrap, post their letters and parcels and perform other tasks. (See Table 17.)

Introductory prompts

Where can I go to buy letter writing materials?
What sort of items would you need to buy?
Do your mum and dad ever go to the post office?
What else can you do at the post office?
Why do we need to write letters?
Are all post offices the same?
What happens when you go there?
How could we set up a post office in the role-play area?
What will we need?

Possible roles

Shop assistant, cashier, customers, post person, letter collector, letter sorter, Postman Pat and characters

Resources

Provide some costumes, leaflets, stamps, money, tills, scales, computer keyboards and VDU monitor, forms, letter writing materials (paper, cards, envelopes, pens, felts, scissors), telephone, desk and chair for assistants, magazines, uniforms.

See Recommended reading for books about post offices.

Link activities

Deal with different aspects of money handling, coin recognition, prices and change.
Produce a variety of correspondence to people.
Write and send real letters to their homes.
Wrap and send various sizes of parcels through the post.
Learn how to sort letters and parcels at the pretend sorting office.
Construct a postbox with signs to give times for collections.

Potential learning opportunities

Personal, social and emotional development

The post office and shop will help children to:

Disposition and attitude

- explore a new role-play area and share previous experiences and information gained about local post office services in the area;

Self-esteem and self-confidence

- show excitement while working together as a team;
- express themselves and show consideration for others while they work and play;
- take on different character roles to explore for themselves a place of work (post office, van driver, sorting office);
- make choices and select materials independently for a task (large box for postbox);

Making relationships/behaviour/self-control

- queue and take their turn and be polite and say please and thank you;
- encourage the ability to choose for themselves by selecting their own materials which are suitable for the task;
- be cooperative and work together considering the feelings of those around them;

- feel confident to ask for help and advice from the post office workers and adults supporting the play;

Sense of community

- develop a sense of belonging to a community by using the local post office to buy stamps and post letters and parcels.

Communication, language and literacy

The post office and shop will help the children to:

Speaking, listening and communicating

- speak clearly and use appropriate body language to communicate with their peers and adults directly or by telephone;
- ask and answer simple questions;
- give complex instructions ('put the little green stamp on the right-hand top corner of the envelope') and ask detailed questions which require explanations;
- use language to take on and recreate familiar roles and experiences;
- learn their own address and postcode;
- use drama to represent stories relating to the post office;

Reading

- take telephone messages and read them back;
- read environmental print on notices, labels, information leaflets and advertisements;
- read lists, letters, postcards, forms, envelopes that other children have written;
- recognise some words connected to the topic (post, stamps, open, closed);
- develop an understanding of the need to be able to read;
- read a selection of relevant fiction and non-fiction books which are available for them to refer to;
- begin to predict what print may say;

Writing

- write names on the forms by using emergent writing and develop through symbols to correct letter formations;
- develop an understanding of the need to be able to write;
- use writing to communicate with others, e.g. send messages, notes, letters, record information and be able to inform others of it;
- send real letters and parcels through the post, taking them to the post office themselves and buying stamps and posting them;
- write their own name and part of their own address on forms and envelopes with adult support.

Mathematical development

The post office and shop will help the children to:

Matching and sorting

- recognise and match 2-D and 3-D shapes (letters and parcels), numerals and letters;

Size, area, shape, space and measure

- measure and select the correct envelopes and wrapping paper for a task, using their understanding of size and area;
- put away and tidy up by using appropriately labelled places (sorting office);
- discuss a letter's journey using positional language;
- compare the weights of three different parcels and put in order of weight using the correct vocabulary;

Number

- recognise numerals in the environment (prices and quantities, door numbers and letters, telephone numbers, stamps and money numbers);
- make telephone directories using simple numbers and their own names;
- count reliably up to ten objects: letters, parcels, stamps, in a variety of settings;

Calculations

- solve simple mathematical problems, counting how many letters altogether, how many are left, up to ten, and simple money problems;
- be familiar with and begin to use language such as more, less, same, when dealing with letters, parcels, money etc.;
- be able to find the total number of objects by combining two sets of money, stamps and parcels;
- use and handle money in the play post office;
- sort and match coins and be able to name most common ones, and begin to understand that each coin has a different value;
- exchange coins for the same value by giving change from cash transactions up to 10p with some adult support;
- know that items are not free and must be paid for by putting prices on the objects to be bought of numerals up to 10p;

Time

- begin to understand the different times of the day, shop opening hours, staff working hours, letter delivery, and begin to order the days of the week.

Knowledge and understanding of the world

The post office and shop will help the children to:

Observe and explore

- explore writing tools and their uses (pens, felts, pencils, cards, labels, paper and envelopes) in the post office;

A sense of place and design and making

- design and construct models for use in the post office (postbox, telephone box, counters, shelves, sorting trays) after visiting a local post office and taking photographs;

A sense of time

- investigate how the postal service has developed and changed over time;

ICT

- investigate how ICT helps communication: telephones, computers, faxes, mobile phones etc.
- have a photo booth where they can take photographs of themselves using a digital camera for identity cards and passports.

Creative development

The post office and shop will help the children to:

Exploring media and materials

- use creative materials to construct and develop the role-play area. Make postboxes, telephone boxes, counter, sorting office etc.;
- make a town out of boxes with house numbers (*Numberlies* characters) and use Roamer as the post person to deliver the post to the correctly numbered house).

Imagination

- act in role as characters in the post office and sorting office;
- retell stories they have heard or watched on video (Postman Pat) and act them out in role;
- create their own stories using the props available and extend the scenario by inventing a problem which they have to solve, e.g. lost letters, puncture, no addresses etc.;

Music

- sing songs and rhymes connected to post people and letters: Postman Pat songs and themes.

Physical development

The post office and shop will help the children to:

Movement

- improve fine and gross motor movements by handling post office materials;
- improve awareness of space by riding post bikes and vans to deliver the post outside;

Using tools and materials

- develop hand-eye coordination by using a variety of tools and materials in the post office;
- develop skills of large construction, decorating and joining materials together, e.g. postbox;
- gain increasing control of clothes and fastenings by dressing up in simple costumes.

Key vocabulary

Postman, letters, postbox, letterbox, uniform, hat, sack, stamps, envelopes, postcards, forms, cheques, pens, large, small, inside, under, over, up, down, next to, choose, collect, cost, money, till, shopping list, please, thank you, photo booth, camera, identity card, passport

Talking points

What do I need to send a letter?
Where can we find them?
What are you going to choose?
What size do you need (bigger, smaller, the same as)?
How much will it cost?
Can you remember what you have bought?
How much change have you got?
Where do you keep your money?
Did you find everything you need?
What does the post person do?
How does he or she find the correct house?
How does he or she get there?
What other ways can you use to send information? (e.g. email, fax, telephone)

Observational focus

Observe and ask the children to show you: Why do we go to the post office? What do we need to do?

1. Cannot remember any significant information/detail ☐
2. Can remember a small amount of information/detail ☐
3. Can give a full account of how and why you would visit a post office ☐
4. Can extend play to create new characters and scenarios ☐

Table 17   Post office

Date	Role play	Shops: Post office	
	Com./lang./lit. development	Mathematical development	Other areas of development
1	Read Postman Pat story and discuss what they will need to set up the area as a post office. The children make simple rules about how they use the area and write them down. What do we use the post office for? Have they ever visited one with their parents?	Sort money, begin to identify coins and notes. Use pennies to count out the value of higher value coins, e.g. 10p. Introduce the idea of time and opening hours. Think about the times of the day, days of the week and months of the year.	Make props, postbox, sorting office, pretend doors with numbers on up to 20. Think about the uniforms postal workers wear.
2	Read posters and leaflets around the post office. Make new posters for Reception Post Office. Write cards and letters to other children. Think about their addresses and put them on envelopes. Buy stamps from the post office and post the letters. Write their names and numbers on forms (ages).	Recognise numbers on stamps and match with coins. Talk about waiting in a queue. Use ordinal numbers. Match and sort letters and envelopes. Count numbers of items of post.	Sort post and deliver it. Discuss the letter's journey (positional language). Use Roamer as a postman to deliver letters to doors with numbers on.
3	Write real letters and take them to the post office, buy stamps and post them. Discuss how long they will take to get there. Tell the story of the letter's	Use the post office as a bank to save money. Write cheques and paying in slips. Understand about credit cards and money machines. Collect child	Emphasise the importance of polite behaviour when you talk and work with people. Introduce a photo booth for the children to take digital

Table 17 *(Contd)*

Date	Role play	Shops: Post office	
	Com./lang./lit. development	Mathematical development	Other areas of development
	journey and sequence.	benefit and pensions, and pay bills, buy car tax and TV licences.	photographs of themselves to put on identity cards.
4	Discuss the other items a post office should sell: pens, paper, cards, envelopes, wrapping paper, sticky tape. Put prices on them. Let the children use the computers to communicate with each other by email.	Send some parcels through the post. Wrap and clearly address them. Think about how heavy they are and how this affects the price of postage. Think about how we weigh objects using scales. Put parcels into order of weight and use the correct comparative language.	Why do we send things through the post (catalogues, mail order and internet shopping)? Go to the computer suite and use the Internet to buy an item.
5	Post offices have telephones. What are they for? Dial telephone numbers, have conversations and think about the advantages of telephones compared to writing a letter.	Write telephone numbers down and pretend to ring them. Use public telephone boxes and compare. How are they different from telephoning from home?	Make a telephone box out of a large box for children to use.

B & Q warehouse

Play situation

Create a shop where children can go and buy items to decorate and mend their property. It comprises a trolley park, car park, shop floor, garden centre, tills and packing area. Children are able to drive their cars, park and go and look around the shop at a variety of tools, decorating materials and garden ware. The children will play roles and begin to understand the processes involved in running a large retail warehouse, and what it might feel like to work there. (See Table 18.)

Introductory prompts

Where can I go to buy DIY materials and tools?
What sort of items would you need to buy?
Do your mum and dad ever decorate their house?
What jobs have you seen them do?
Why do we keep our homes nice?
Do you care what your bedroom looks like?
How is a warehouse different to a small hardware shop?
What happens when you get there?
How could we set up a warehouse in the role-play area?
What will we need?

Possible roles

Shop assistants, craftsmen/women, customers, shelf stackers, cashier, car park attendants, enquiry advisors and Bob the Builder's friends

Resources

Supply the shop with costumes, leaflets, colour charts, telephone, writing tools and paper, desk, chairs, magazines, tools, paint pots, brushes, rollers, plastic trays, wood, plastic, metal, real tools, nails, screws, nuts, trolleys, baskets, tills, money, receipts, Brio and other construction kits, catalogues, boxes, garden goods.

See Recommended reading for books about house building.

Link activities

Make a catalogue of tools and wallpaper for the children to sell.
Recognise and match shapes, tools, colours, numbers, words connected with the B & Q warehouse.
Make Bob the Builder's yard and office and retell some of the stories.
Build walls and lay tiles in the role-play house, tessellating shapes and making patterns.
Take telephone messages, orders and enquiries from the house.

Potential learning opportunities

Personal, social and emotional development

The B & Q warehouse will help children to:

Disposition and attitudes

- explore and enjoy while they play in the new role-play area and share experiences with other children who have visited a DIY warehouse with their parents;

Self-confidence and self-esteem

- express themselves confidently and show consideration for other children they work with;
- feel confident to ask for help and advice from shop workers and adults supporting the play;
- take on different character roles to explore themselves and a place of work;

Making relationships/behaviour/self-control

- learn to form queues, take their turn fairly and be polite and say please and thank you while they play;
- choose their own materials independently and ensure they are suitable for the task in question: brushes, rollers and paint for painting, bricks and cement for building;
- understand that everyone has different needs and be cooperative, listen to others, work together and consider the feelings of those around them.

Communication, language and literacy

Speaking, listening and communicating

The B & Q warehouse will help children to:

- speak clearly and use appropriate body language to communicate with peers and adults directly or by telephone;
- give complex instructions and explanations, and to ask and answer detailed questions about stock that is available in the warehouse;
- develop an understanding of questions using: how, when, where and why;
- use language to take on and recreate familiar roles in the role-play, e.g. customer, sales assistant;

Reading and linking sounds and letters

- read environmental print, notices, labels and price lists, be able to give information about the goods and recognise some words connected to the topic;
- read catalogues and other relevant fiction and non-fiction books related to B & Q which are readily available around the area;
- listen to a range of stories and poems and use role-play / drama to act them out;
- read back messages and information they have written down from telephone conversations or information found in catalogues;

Writing

- understand the need to write as a means of communication;
- write down messages, labels and shopping lists around the warehouse using the displays and books as clues, with emergent writing which may develop through symbols to correct letter formation.

Mathematical development

The B & Q warehouse will help children to:

Matching and sorting

- sort and match tools, coins and materials using colour size and shape and begin to identify the common properties of materials to sort shop merchandise;

Number

- recognise, match and name some numerals in the warehouse environment on notices, signs, price tags and labels, and relate to them;
- count reliably up to ten objects (e.g. nails) and beyond in the warehouse;
- predict how many washers or other items will fit in a box;
- begin to record numbers for prices and quantity;
- use number rhymes and poems to complement activities, e.g. 'Peter hammers with one hammer';

Calculations

- solve simple mathematical problems in real situations;
- begin to use language such as more, less, the same as, in play;
- begin to find the total number of objects, for example, combining the contents of two shopping trolleys;
- introduce the idea that items are not free and must be paid for by the children putting on price tags up to 10p;
- understand and use and handle money in the play situation;
- name most common coins and begin to understand that each coin has a different value;
- begin to exchange coins for the same value in giving change from cash transactions;

Shape and space and measure

- match and sort 2-D and 3-D shapes and real objects: tools, coins, using a number of criteria;
- investigate tessellation using tiles, bricks and other shapes recording the different patterns that form;
- begin to identify the properties of shapes and how this will help in construction projects;
- plan, construct and evaluate models and patterns: wallpaper, paving and walls;
- measure and select the correct materials and tools with each child having a tape measure, ruler and pieces of string;
- use positional language when setting up the warehouse, putting away and tidying up tools and materials by using the appropriate labelled boxes and shelves;

Size and area

- develop an awareness of the size and area of objects, and how this will affect the way they use them;

Length, weight, capacity/volume

- be aware of the length, weight and capacity of items for sale in the warehouse;

Time

- understand the times of the day and shop opening hours: be able to use a play clock with open and closed signs.

Knowledge and understanding of the world

The B & Q warehouse will help children to:

Observe and explore

- observe what their own home and school look like, beginning to identify different parts of the buildings;
- develop curiosity and interest in the buildings around their local environment and compare their appearances and functions;
- observe and investigate the tools and materials they find in the warehouse;

Materials and their properties

- tell different materials apart, identify their properties (waterproofing or strength) and begin to recognise some common ones by name: glass, bricks, sand, wood, plastic, metal etc.;

Design and making

- help to plan and design the warehouse;
- explore real tools and their uses during practical projects;
- investigate tools that require power and think about why;
- build toy and real walls using cement and record the changes and the patterns the bricks make;
- design, make and decorate a house/box unit that they can play in;

Sense of time and place

- talk about their homes and how they differ from ones in different countries or ones built long ago;
- design a room from the *Peepo!* book (pre-war) and a modern room and compare the two;

Creative development

The B & Q warehouse will help children to:

Exploring media and materials

- use creative materials to decorate the role-play area;
- use a wide variety of materials to do observation work on old and new tools, walls and buildings;
- recreate patterns on buildings by printing;
- use creative materials to create the role-play area;

Making

- make box rooms to represent a room today and one 100 years ago;

Imagination

- use the props to support their play effectively;
- act out roles to represent a real situation in the warehouse;
- retell a story they have heard, e.g. about 'Bob the Builder', connected to the topic, play cooperatively with their peers and act out an invented story using the props available;

Music

- sing rhymes and songs related to homes and buildings: *'Okki-tokki-unga'*, 'The wise man and the foolish man';
- use instruments freely to complement the singing.

Physical development

The B & Q warehouse will help children to:

- improve fine and gross motor control by using tools, construction kits and building materials, and develop hand-eye coordination;
- use tools to write shopping lists etc;
- move freely from one area to another;
- pack bought goods and transport them home.

Talking points

In the car park

Can you find a parking space?
When packing up your car, is there enough space for the goods you have purchased?
Why do you think cars are useful?

In the warehouse

What do you think you need?
Where can we find them?
What are you going to choose and why?
What colours are there? Do you like them? Do they match?
What size do you need?
Where do you keep your money when you shop?
How much will it cost?
How much change did you get?
Can you remember what you have bought?
Did you find everything you needed?

Key vocabulary

Large, small, inside, under, over, up, down, next to, choose, paint, brushes, collect, rollers, trays, price, bargain, price list, catalogue, tool names, garden equipment, money, till, shopping list, please, thank you

Observational focus

Observe and ask the children to show you why they needed to go the warehouse. What did they need to do when they got there?

1. Cannot remember any significant information or detail ☐

2. Can remember a small amount of information/detail ☐
3. Can give a full account of how and why you would visit a warehouse ☐
4. Can extend play to create new characters and scenarios ☐

Table 18   DIY shop

Date	Role play	Shops: B & Q warehouse	
	Com./lang./lit. development	Mathematical development	Other areas of development
1	Discuss what happens when you go to the shops to buy goods to decorate with. Has anyone been to B & Q? What sort of things does it sell? Small groups looking at a catalogue.	Look at tools for sale and match them to outlines. Make sets of tools that are the same.	Learn the names and some of the functions of the tools for sale.
2	Discuss what tools look like and what they are used for. Play mystery and guessing games.	Begin to set up the shop. Talk about shelving and where goods will be placed and why using positional language.	Cut out pictures of tools and make a catalogue for the class B & Q warehouse showing what is available.
3	Discuss the roles with the children and begin to act out what happens when you go into a warehouse. Have some adult support available if required.	Introduce money and the price of goods. Write prices in the catalogue. Make a price list to display. Label individual goods that are for sale.	Make large collages of B & Q workers noting the colours of their uniforms.
4	Discuss the roles with the children and begin to act out what happens when you go into a warehouse. Have some adult support if required.	Children make price tags all under 10p.	Look at real tools and try using them. Make observational pictures of them.
5	Discuss the roles with the children and begin to act out what happens when you go into a warehouse.	Children use Brio construction kits to test tools. How many nuts can I undo in one minute etc.? Record how they get on.	Look at real tools and try using them. Make observational pictures of them. Discuss with the children about having a trip to the local B & Q.
6	What do we need to decorate our house? Add paints, brushes, rollers to warehouse on	Look at the different sizes of brushes and tins of paint. Use the correct mathematical language	Learn the names and functions of the new tools introduced to the warehouse.

Table 18 *(Contd)*

Date	Role play	Shops: B & Q warehouse	
	Com./lang./lit. development	Mathematical development	Other areas of development
	labelled shelves. Read *Oh No! Peedie Peebles* and discuss how her house is decorated.	when comparing them. In the water tray investigate different coloured waters and different sized containers.	
7	Discuss what the new tools are used for. Why do they think rollers are better than brushes for large jobs? Sequence the 'Peebles' story using coloured paints and paper acting out the story and decorating as they go.	Put tins of paint in the correct position on the labelled shelves. Compare using brushes and rollers to cover a large area. Decorate a large box room using them.	The children begin to mix colours together to make new ones using: paints, inks, dough and coloured water.
8	Help the children choose their roles and encourage them to go to the warehouse and choose wallpaper, glue and other materials they need to hang wallpaper.	Let the children price the new decorating goods and make a comprehensive price list. Let them predict how many pieces of wallpaper they will need to cover their box room. Act in role to buy wallpaper: Mum, Dad, adviser and cashier.	Transfer the new colours onto a colour chart for customers to choose their paint from. Experiment with simple printing patterns.
9	Decide on roles and begin to act out what happens when you visit the warehouse. Add colour charts and discuss the importance of matching colours.	Children make clear price tags for the goods matching the prices on the list. Encourage them to match colours, shapes and designs.	Introduce patterns on other household items: carpets and tiles. Let the children make tessellating patterns with different shaped tiles: squares, rectangles, triangles and hexagons.
10	Let the children decide which roles they will play and pretend to go to the warehouse to purchase paints, wallpaper and the tools they will need to complete the job.	Encourage the children to play independently with the tools, materials and money.	Make patterns to cover carpets using printing as a medium and make them available for sale in the warehouse.
11	Continue to use the B & Q warehouse to	Add 3-D items into the shop: bricks etc. and let	Go around school and look closely at different

Table 18   *(Contd)*

Date	Role play	Shops: B & Q warehouse	
	Com../lang./lit. development	Mathematical development	Other areas of development
	buy and sell goods independently. Write shopping lists, price tags etc. using the props in the warehouse to assist them.	the children price them. Try building with toy bricks and discuss how they stay together.	walls. What patterns can they see? Make a building site using a large sand tray with diggers and little people.
12	Read *Little Lumpty* story to the children and discuss the characters. Discuss rhymes and stories where walls occur.	Count out bricks and predict how many they will need to build a wall for Humpty. Use large constructions outdoors.	Use real bricks and cement and build small walls with the children. Make sure the children understand safety issues: washing hands and being careful with the heavy bricks. Children can record the changes they see.
13	Let the children read *Little Lumpty* again independently and sequence the story. Discuss rhymes and stories where walls occur.	Encourage the children to use money independently, reading price lists and labels.	Printed wall patterns. Children investigate which type is the strongest.
14	Discuss the different materials you can find in B & Q. Have a look around the classroom and outside to see if you can find any of them.	Make sets of objects using the materials they are made with as the criteria for sorting.	Look at the properties of materials you find in buildings and discuss them. Make observational pictures of them in sets, for example a mirror and a window are both made of glass.
15	Discuss the different materials you can find in B & Q. Have a look around the classroom and outside to see if you can find any of them.	Make sets of objects using the materials they are made of as criteria for sorting.	Make creative works using different materials.
16	Continue to use B & Q warehouse for buying and selling goods. Introduce *Bob the Builder* and read one of the stories. Begin to set up his office to take	Telephone number for Bob's office. Make a telephone directory of numbers, one for each child and adult that the children make up.	Make large life-size collages of Bob's friends using a wide range of materials with the children drawing the characters.

Table 18 *(Contd)*

Date	Role play	Shops: B & Q warehouse	
	Com./lang./lit. development	Mathematical development	Other areas of development
	orders and deliveries of materials (telephone, typewriter, computer, writing tools, cards and paper).		
17	Read another *Bob the Builder* story. Sequence the story and encourage the children to act it out. Discuss the sort of jobs Bob and his friends have to do.	Dial Bob using the school intercom system. Count out his equipment e.g. screws, nuts and nails.	Make patterned wallpaper for Bob to use. Put samples in a book for customers to select the one they like best.
18	Read the story of Bob building a house. Recall the order in which things happen.	Lay tiles in a kitchen or outside with paving stones. What have they got to think about? (shape, materials and size). Try using carpet tile shapes.	Print more wallpaper patterns, and decide which one should cost the most, which one should cost the least? Why?
19	Discuss the different materials and tools you find in the warehouse. Watch a *Bob the Builder* video and compare with books.	Lay tiles in a kitchen or outside with paving stones. What have they got to think about? (shape, materials and size). Try using carpet tile shapes.	Play independently in the warehouse and Bob's office.
20	Discuss the roles that can be chosen with the children and begin to act out what happens when you visit Bob.	Play freely using appropriate mathematical language to discuss number, size, colour, shape and order.	Make creative pictures and models using different materials the children can find in the warehouse and office.

Cafe

Play situation

Create a cafe where people can go and buy items to eat and drink while away from home. It comprises a counter to serve customers, tills, a kitchen area and telephones to take orders. Customers are able to come in and order hot and cold food from a menu, sit down at a table to eat it, receive a bill and pay for it. The cafe will contain real and pretend food and drinks. It will also offer a delivery service for telephone orders and take-away meals. Consider serving food from other countries and cultures such as Chinese, Italian or Indian. (See Tables 19 and 20.)

Introductory prompts

Where can we go if we are hungry?
What sort of items would we buy there?
Do you ever go to cafes with your mum and dad?
Where do we eat in school?
How do we get our food?
Where can we go to try different kinds of food?
What jobs have to be done in a cafe/restaurant?
Is a cafe kitchen different to the one in your house?
We have a big kitchen in school, what is it used for?
What happens when you go there?
How could we set up a cafe or restaurant in the role-play area?
What will we need?

Possible roles

Cafe assistants, cook, chefs, waiter, washing up staff, customers, cashier, delivery bikers

Resources

Equip your cafe with plates, cups, carriers, dishes, cutlery, straws, napkins, chopsticks, woks, shop window, till, purses, money, telephone, tables, chairs, food, menus, food pictures, adverts, blackboard for daily specials, writing tools for taking orders, plastic food, aprons, caps and uniforms, litter bins.
See Recommended reading for books about cafes.

Link activities

Make a menu and posters with the different types of food that the children would like to sell.
Recognise and match shapes, tools, colours, numbers and words connected with food.
Recognise and make different types of food out of dough.
Discuss and compare how different types of food are cooked.
Think about what we are going to use to eat the food with: knives, forks, spoons, chopsticks or fingers.
Cook a banquet with the children and encourage them to eat a variety of food.
Think about what is healthy to eat. Collect sets of healthy food and sets of unhealthy food.
Make telephone orders from the role-play house to the cafe using the intercom telephones.
Deal with money, prices and packing food for the customer.

Potential learning opportunities

The role-play cafe will help the children to:

Personal, social and emotional development

Disposition and attitude

- explore new learning opportunities in the cafe and share other children's experiences who have visited one with parents;
- enjoy themselves with their friends and supporting adults and begin to reflect on their play experiences;

Self-confidence and self-esteem

- express themselves clearly and confidently while showing consideration for others when ordering food from the cafe staff or waiting in queues;

Making relationships/behaviour/self-control

- be cooperative, work together, understand that people have different needs and consider the feelings of those around them;
- take on different character roles to explore themselves and a place of work;
- be polite and say please and thank you to assistants and waitresses;

Self-care

- wash their hands before eating;
- choose for themselves confidently, by selecting their own food from the menu;
- eat politely using knives, forks, spoons and chopsticks, and follow simple table manners;

Sense of community

- appreciate that other people have different customs and beliefs, religions, languages, festivals and to respect and respond positively to them;
- visit a local cafe, restaurant or take-away and know how to order food.

Communication, language and literacy

The role-play cafe will help the children to:

Speaking, listening and communicating

- speak clearly and use appropriate body language to get attention, to defend their own interests and to be understood by friends and family;

- develop their questioning techniques and ability to give complex instructions about what food is available and how much it costs;
- take telephone messages and read them back;
- use language to take on and create familiar roles and experiences (waitress, diner);

Reading

- read and write notices and labels and menus for the cafe giving information about foods and their prices;
- read from a selection of relevant fiction and non-fiction books available to refer to;

Writing

- write orders for items of food they would like to buy and read them back to the customers and the kitchen staff;
- write their names and the food they require in the order book;
- use emergent writing and develop through symbols to correct letter formation to recognise and write words connected to the topic.

Mathematical development

The role-play cafe will help the children to:

Matching, sorting and shape

- sort and match food and table settings using colour, size and shape;
- tidy up and put away food in appropriately labelled places;

Number

- identify numbers in the environment on signs, labels etc;
- count reliably and accurately up to ten pieces of food around the cafe and develop an ability to estimate;
- recognise numbers on signs and menu and relate them to money;

Calculations

- use number rhymes and poems to complement activities, e.g. 'Five currant buns'.
- begin to solve simple mathematical problems in the cafe;
- be familiar with and begin to use the correct mathematical language: more than, less than and the same as;
- find the total number of objects combining food items on two plates (sets);
- use and handle money confidently in the cafe, be able to name most common coins and be aware of their value;

- exchange coins for the same value and give change from cash transactions;
- know that items of food are not free and must be paid for, by putting on price labels of numerals up to 10p;

Measuring size, length, weight, capacity and volume

- understand that you can weigh objects to see how heavy they are using scales and other measures, and compare them using the correct mathematical language;
- use different sizes and types of containers to explore capacity, comparing them using the correct mathematical language while making drinks etc.;

Time

- know the different times of the day, cafe opening hours and staff working hours.

Knowledge and understanding of the world

The role-play cafe will help the children to:

Observe and investigate

- visit a cafe, fast food outlet or restaurant and record what they need;
- show an interest in the new cafe project and offer suggestions about props and costumes which will complement their play;

Materials and their properties

- recognise, describe and name different types of food;
- explore and investigate what happens to food when its temperature changes;
- develop skills in using new tools for eating and cooking;
- recognise the need for care and safety while they prepare food and work in the kitchen;

Design and making

- plan and design the cafe area;
- name some tools that require power to complete cooking jobs very quickly;
- understand the danger of using electricity when in the kitchen;

ICT

- use ICT to make cafe pictures and decorate the cafe with them: My World 'Cafe' and Granada Learning 'Cafe';
- use computerised cooking ovens and microwaves;
- develop an awareness of time when thinking about work, meals and timetables.

Creative development

The role-play cafe will help the children to:

Exploring media and materials

- make coloured posters of food using different tools and materials.
- make models of food for sale in the cafe using *Okki-tokki-unga*, 'Ten fat sausages', 'Eat brown bread', 'I'm a little teapot'; *Bingo Lingo*, 'Teatime Treats'; *Me*, 'Sweet Potato', 'I'm So Hot', 'Food Wrap', 'Jelly Belly'.

Imagination

- act out roles and create stories using the props available;
- develop scenarios and create problems for the children to solve within the role-play house.

Physical development

The role-play cafe will help the children to:

Movement and sense of space

- move freely from one area to another;

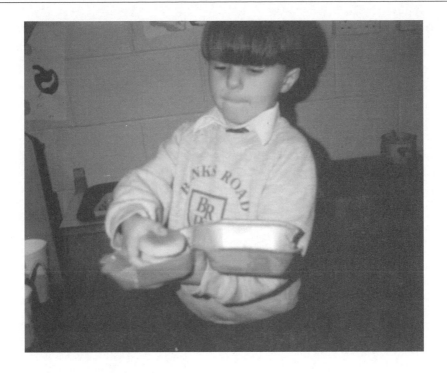

- balance goods on trays;
- use tools and materials to make things for the area;
- use tools to eat and cook with: knives, forks, spoons or chopsticks;
- use tools to write with;
- pack and deliver food to customers.

Key vocabulary

food names, plates, cups, hot, cold, order, choose, menu, portion, please, thank you, apron, uniform, box, packet, bike

Talking points

What are you going to choose?
How much will it cost?
What would you like to eat?
What words will they use?
Can the waiter repeat the order?
Can you match the food with the order?
What can you give to someone who does not eat meat?
What is the most popular meal?
How are you going to cook the food?
Can the server remember who ordered?
Are you happy with the food?
Do you need anything else?
Can we have the bill, please?
Can I take the food out, e.g. takeaways?

Observational focus

Observe and ask the children to show you: What do they go to the cafe for?
What do they need to do?

1. Cannot remember any significant information/detail ☐
2. Can remember a small amount of information/detail ☐
3. Can give a full account of how and why you would visit a cafe ☐
4. Can extend play to create new characters and scenarios ☐

Table 19   Cafe

Date	Role play	Shops: Cafe	
	Com./lang./lit. development	Mathematical development	Other areas of development
1	Discuss what goes on in a cafe. What areas will they need: kitchen, counter and eating area? What kind of food are we going to serve? What kind of food do the children enjoy eating?	Set out the tables with patterned cloths. Put the place mats on the tables with the matching coloured knives, forks, spoons, cups, plates, dishes and add sauces, salt, pepper, vinegar. Match the correct number of chairs to each place setting.	Use play food confidently. Make pretend shaped biscuits and cakes to sell in the cafe. Make real shaped biscuits and cakes to serve in the cafe. Discuss table manners.
2	Make a menu of the food the children would like to eat. Use	Decide on a price for the foods. Make labels and signs. Pour lots of	Make shaped sandwiches with different fillings to serve

Table 19   *(Contd)*

Date	Role play	Shops: Cafe	
	Com./lang./lit. development	Mathematical development	Other areas of development
	pictures and writing. Make boards with daily specials on.	coloured drinks into different-sized cups and decide whether cups are empty, full or half full.	in the cafe. Make a real a cup of tea.
3	Ask and answer questions concerning the food. Have a waiter to take orders back to the kitchen. Remember the importance of polite behaviour and manners.	Write down orders noting how many of each item is required and the table number.	Play independently in a traditional cafe using tea sets, play food etc.
4	Has anyone visited a fast food restaurant? Discuss what happens there. How is it different from a traditional cafe?	Count out the food items and ensure the orders match.	Think about fast food. Make some dough burgers, fish, chips etc. Think about what containers you will use to keep it hot.
5	Develop the idea of ordering on the phone and delivering the hot food to people's houses by using pretend cars and bikes outside delivering to numbered houses.	Discuss routes to people's homes and which is the quickest. Discuss the directions they have to go. What could happen if they got stuck in a traffic jam?	If you eat takeaway food, litter must be put in a bin.

Table 20   Chinese restaurant

Date	Role play	Shops: Chinese restaurant	
	Com./lang./lit. development	Mathematical development	Other areas of development
1	Discuss what goes on in a restaurant, and why we have them. What kind of food are we going to serve? Are the children familiar with some items of Chinese food and have any of them tasted it before?	Set out the tables with red and gold patterned cloths. Put the place mats on the tables with the chopsticks, spoons, cups, bowls, sauces, salt, pepper and soy sauce. Match chairs to settings.	Make real and pretend food for the restaurant using traditional Chinese cooking implements: wok and chopsticks.

Table 20 *(Contd)*

Date	Role play	Shops: Chinese restaurant	
	Com./lang./lit. development	Mathematical development	Other areas of development
2	Make a menu of the Chinese food the children would like to eat (use a menu from a restaurant). Use pictures, photographs and writing. Make boards with specials on using Chinese writing. Children begin to take on the roles of the characters in the play situation.	Decide on a price for the various foods. Make labels and signs with pictures and prices.	Look at menus from Chinese restaurants and discuss them. Use chopsticks starting with crisps then moving on to noodles and more complex food stuffs.
3	Ask and answer questions concerning food. Explain what certain dishes are. Have a waiter to take orders back to the kitchen. Encourage the kitchen staff to check the orders carefully reading the waiter's writing.	Write down orders noting how many of each item is required.	Experiment with red drinks considering the size of drink containers and whether cups are empty, full or half full.
4	Discuss what foods we would need to make a banquet and write a shopping list. Go and buy products (pretend to shop for them).	Check you have ordered enough food and equipment for your group, e.g. six prawn crackers for six children, 12 chopsticks for six children.	Cook prawn crackers with a supporting adult and watch them grow while they cook.
5	Read recipes and cook real food following the instructions carefully.	Count, weigh and measure food before it is cooked.	Encourage the children to act as real waiters and serve their friends the special Chinese food. Children try to use chopsticks to eat with.

Vet's surgery, pet shop and zoo

Play situation

Create a vet's surgery, waiting room and a pet shop. The children will play the roles of staff and patients and some toy animals will be included. The children will begin to understand why they take their pets to the vet's and what equipment and care they require to be looked after effectively. They need to know how to make appointments.

This can be extended outdoors by making a safari park with toy vehicles moving around viewing animal pens or a zoo. (See Table 21–23.)

Introductory prompts

Where do we go if our animals are sick?
What do we think the vet will do?
Do any other people work at the vet's surgery?
Why do we need to make an appointment?
Can anyone else help animals if they are sick or injured?
What happens in the pet shop?
What products does it sell and why?
Has anybody visited a zoo or safari park?
What did you see there?

Possible roles

Vets, animal nurses, RSPCA workers, receptionist, animal patients and owners, radiographers, shopkeeper, farmers, zookeepers, kiosk operators

Resources

Supply your role-play area with a surgery, waiting room with chairs, pets, shop, posters, magazines, appointments book, animal cards, clock, calendar, writing tools, record cards, doctor/vet's tools, table, torches, bottles, spoons, tins, prescription pads, operating theatre, X-ray machine, X-rays, toy animals, animal leaflets, construction for fencing and making animal shelters.

See Recommended reading for books about vets, pets and zoos.

Link activities

Make collage of vets and nurses and give them identities.
Make models and pictures of different animals and identify the various parts discussing what some of them do.
Look at paw and footprints and be creative and mathematical.
Discuss children's experiences of visiting the vet's, dogs' homes and pet shops.
Think about what makes animals healthy: water, food, exercise, contentment and love.
Collect a selection of healthy animal food and chat about it.

Potential learning opportunities

Personal, social and emotional development

The animal role-play scenarios help children to:

Disposition and attitudes

- explore new learning environments and share experiences other children have had when they visited a vet, pet shop, zoo or safari park;
- enjoy themselves with their friends and supporting adults and begin to reflect on their play experiences;

Self-confidence and self-esteem

- improve their confidence and begin to develop their own personal character and personality;
- develop personal qualities such as imagination, creativity, confidence, humour and perseverance while developing the animal play scenario;

Making relationships/behaviour/self-control

- express feelings (nervousness, sadness or fear) and be sensitive to the needs of other people or animals, being able to recognise and comfort a child or animal who is distressed or sick;
- share limited space fairly so that their play can develop, they can take turns, develop self-made rules of behaviour and improve their ability to work as a member of a group;
- develop a caring attitude towards others and modify their own actions in consideration of other living creatures;

Self-care

- develop an awareness of their own personal needs, personal hygiene and be able to take off and put on clothes (costumes) with increasing independence;
- select appropriate equipment independently for a task and use it sensibly, feeling confident to ask for help from a familiar adult or peer;

Sense of community

- treat animals with respect and to care for them in a responsible way so they do not affect the rest of our community: dogs wandering the streets, inoculating them and preventing them from having lots of young;
- understand that animal care workers are an important part of the local community and invite the People's Dispensary for Sick Animals (PDSA) to visit school.

Communication, language and literacy

The animal role-play scenarios help children to:

Speaking, listening and communicating

- speak clearly using appropriate body language to get attention, to defend their own interests and to communicate with adults and children in the vet's, zoo or pet shop;
- be able to name animals, equipment and other vocabulary relevant to the topic;
- develop questioning techniques using how, when, where, and why, and begin to use language as a means of communicating, giving simple instructions, asking for help and expressing opinions;
- respond and use appropriate social conventions: please and thank you;
- respond to aural stimuli using the telephone to make appointments, find out names, ages, addresses and problems with the animals;

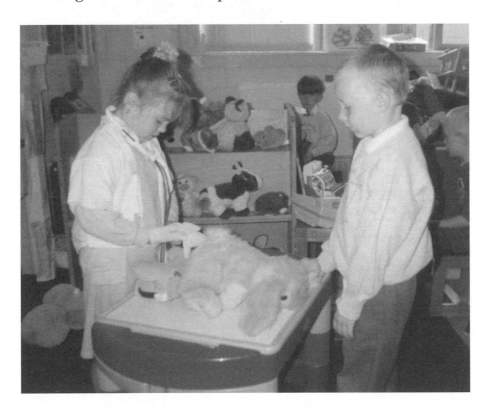

Reading

- share stories about animals and develop their need to be able to read;
- read environmental print around the role-play area by reading magazines, signs, leaflets, posters and non-fiction books about animals and the people who work with them, beginning to recognise some key words;
- read back information the vet or receptionist has written about the sick animals or notices on enclosures referring to different animals;

Writing

- write down children's name, animal's name, addresses, ages, in a way that can be reread using symbolic writing through to conventional letter forms;
- record what the vet can see in pictorial or written form: animal-shaped record cards;
- write shopping lists to take to the pet shop for pets, equipment and animal feed they need to buy;

- write leaflets and posters about how to look after animals properly and safely, developing confidence and enjoyment in writing.

Mathematical development

The animal role-play scenarios help children to:

Matching, sorting and shape

- match the shapes of vet's tools and always return them to the correct position on clearly labelled shelves;

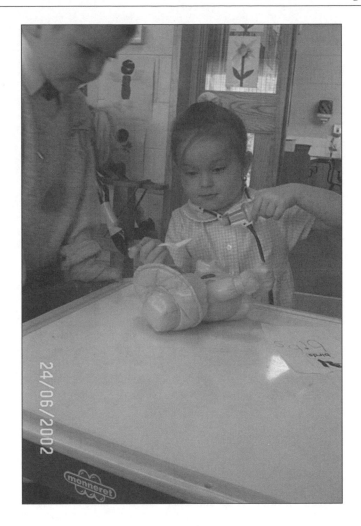

- match animals and feed to the correct box, cage or shelf using labels with pictures and clearly written words;
- group animals into sets considering a number of attributes:

Number

- use numerals to inform us of an animal's age;
- count the animals present and order them using ordinal numbers: those waiting for an operation;

Calculations

- count reliably the number of body parts on an animal: legs, tails, ears or beaks. Then count them on a number of animals. Develop the skills of counting in 2s, 4s and 5s;
- add sets of animals, food and money together to find a total: hamsters and birds;
- use and read money labels on price lists, goods and services in the shop, vet's or zoo;

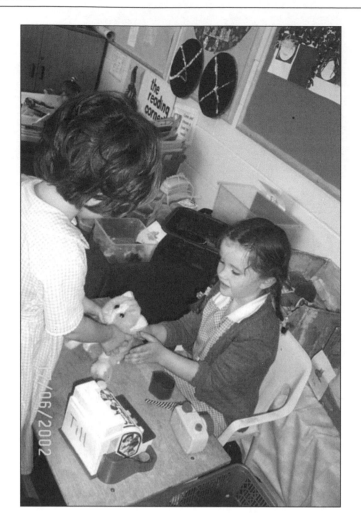

Length, weight, capacity and volume

- explore the ideas of capacity using small units of measurement: spoonfuls for medicine;
- begin to understand that you can weigh objects to see how heavy they are: animal feed at the pet shop, animals' weight at the vet's;

Time

- understand the times of the day: morning, afternoon and night, and begin to identify the days of the week;
- understand the importance of having watches and clocks so that we can tell the time accurately enabling us to get to places on time.

Knowledge and understanding of the world

The animal role-play scenarios help children to:

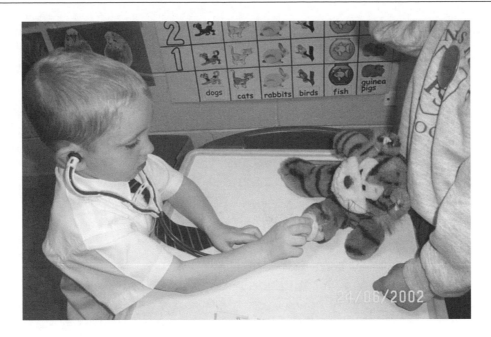

Observe and explore/life processes and living things

- observe and use their sense of touch to discover the new textures you find on different animals: fur, scales and feathers, and discuss their observations and investigations they carried out and how they recorded the number of legs, fur, scales or feathers;
- have some knowledge of the organs inside animals, e.g. brain, heart, lungs, digestive tract;
- understand the differing needs and characteristics of living things to keep them healthy;
- show care and consideration to living things;
- understand aspects of the environment that certain animals live in naturally;
- develop an awareness of some of the differences and similarities between animals;

Design and making

- design and make resources for the role-play area: notices, models of animals, animal homes, props for pet shop and cages. Visit a local pet shop, zoo, safari park or vet's to get some ideas;

Sense of time and place

- make zig-zag books to show an awareness of the passage of time as baby animals grow and change into adults.

ICT

- use ICT to complement their learning: CD–ROMs 'At the vet's', 'Patch the Puppy', 'Fetch the Vet';
- use Roamer or other programmable toy pretending to be an animal.

Creative development

The animal role-play scenarios help children to:

Exploring media and materials

- create observation work based on animals using a variety of media;
- use a variety of media and tools to create collages of vets, nurses and other staff and give them identities;
- make posters and information pictures for the role-play area;
- design and make junk models and pictures of different animals using a variety of materials and techniques;

Music

- listen to and join in with songs and rhymes about their animals: 'How much is that doggie in the window?';
- use simple instruments to complement their performances;

Imagination

- use drama to recreate what it is like to go to the vet's surgery, zoo, safari park or pet shop;
- create scenarios about familiar events and try to solve problems;
- pretend to be different animals in role and think carefully about any special features they may have.

Physical development

The animal role-play scenarios help children to:

Movements

- improve fine and gross motor movements while they work in the role-play area;
- use a wide range of tools and materials to develop their coordination while they set up the area and use it;
- pretend to be different animals by being able to balance and move different body parts;

Health and bodily awareness

- name different parts of an animal's body and begin to understand some of their functions;
- recognise the need for personal hygiene when handling and caring for any animals.

Talking points

What pet would you like to own and why?
Do you think it will cost a lot of money to care for?
What is the pet owner's name, address, age?
What is your pet called etc.?
What is the matter with it?
How do you think the animal feels?
Who would you like to see?
What time/day would you like to come?
Why does the vet examine it?
What food does your pet eat?
Where do you go to get your pet's medicines?
How much will they cost?
What will happen to them?
When can I come and see my pet?
How many patients have they seen?
Can they fit one more patient in?
Have you ever been to the vet's?
What do you think your pet's bones are for?
What happens if your pet breaks one?
Has your pet ever had an operation?
How did you travel to the zoo or safari park?
What animals did you see?

Key vocabulary

Vets, nurses, staff, cages, enclosures, pet carriers, stethoscope, tablets, medicines, spoons, injections, care, gentle, scales, weight, sale, money, feeds, food and water bowls, equipment, leads, cat flaps, animals, cats, dogs, rabbits, guinea pigs, hamsters, fish, spiders, snakes, horses, goats, zoo animals and more

Observational focus

Observe and ask the children to show you what happens at the vet's/pet shop or zoo.

1. Cannot remember any significant information/detail ☐
2. Can remember a small amount of information and detail ☐
3. Can give a full account of how to go to a vet's, zoo and a pet shop ☐
4. Can extend play to create new characters and scenarios ☐

Table 21   Vet's surgery

Date	Role play	Shops: Vet's	
	Com./lang./lit. development	Mathematical development	Other areas of development
1	Discuss setting up the area as a vet's and discover if the children already know about visiting vet's and animals. Encourage the children to think what equipment they will need for props, rules that apply when playing, the number of children involved and roles to be played. What jobs can they do in the area?	Use shape, colour and texture to create the new area. Think about the size of the animals and order them. Make an equipment shadow grid (vet's medical tools). Think where numbers are useful and display them. Sort and match groups of animals.	Make props, create a surgery, waiting room and pet shop, decorated with children's own pictures of animals. Think about safety and hygiene when handling animals.
2	Read posters, animal cards, books and leaflets around role-play area. Make new posters to show how to care for animals. Try reading fiction and non-fiction books about animals using picture cues. Sequence them so the events occur in the correct order. Make cards to explain what you do at the vet's.	Count animals and discuss their ages. Think of number rhymes connected to animals. Count the number of legs that animals have and record them. Animal washing on line (numbered 0–20).	Use ICT to record children's own pets: photographs and simple databases. Create lots of observational pictures and oral descriptions of what different animals look like.
3	Collect the relevant props and act out a visit to a vet's with a sick animal. Watch television programmes and read stories: *Animal Hospital*, *The Vets*, and *Mog Visits the Vet's*.	Draw pictures of animals looking at the patterns on their bodies. Try to recreate these patterns using different media.	The importance of polite behaviour when they talk and work with people. Respect what others say and listen carefully to them. Show care and consideration to sick animals and their owners who may be very emotional.
4	Extend this by recording with a tape or writing down what the vet said and begin to make records of the	Make homes for animals using bricks so the animal fits inside snugly. Discuss size and begin to use comparative	Think about how larger animals are kept in farms and zoos and some of the problems that might arise. How

102

Table 21   *(Contd)*

Date	Role play	Shops: Vet's	
	Com./lang./lit. development	Mathematical development	Other areas of development
	animals' visits using animal shaped cards.	language.	do they measure medicines and tablets? Use injections and spoons to measure small amounts of liquids.
5	Start to use an appointment book. Act out what it would be like to do an operation or give an X-ray to a sick animal.	Think about times of the day. Write telephone numbers down and pretend to ring them. Introduce the idea of having to pay for treatment and using coins etc.	Discuss the sort of emergencies that a vet may be called out to. Let the children tell one in role outside in the play yard, e.g. 'A dog is run over, what do think might happen next?'

Table 22   Pet shop

Date	Role play	Shops: Pet shop	
	Com./lang./lit. development	Mathematical development	Other areas of development
1	Introduce a big book about the pet shop. Has any child been to one? Discuss what it sells, who works there and how we can set one up in the classroom: soft toy animals, till, cages, animal feed and money.	Match animals to pictures. Put labels and prices on the trays and cages. Count the different kinds of animals: dogs, cats, mice, birds, snakes, spiders, guinea pigs, rabbits and fish.	Make cages, tanks and boxes for the pets. Discuss animal homes in the wild and the ones animals have as pets.
2	Discuss roles of the shopkeeper, customer and animal carer. Think about what they will say to each other. Write shopping lists and take them to the shop. Make displays and price labels to identify goods for sale.	Look and count the number of legs the animals have and record your findings.	Use bedding, stones and sand to make the cages ready for the animals.
3	Investigate non-fiction books, posters and	Let the children make labels and price the	Discuss why every animal's feed is

Table 22   *(Contd)*

Date	Role play	Shops: Pet shop	
	Com./lang./lit. development	Mathematical development	Other areas of development
	leaflets about pets and how to care for them. Encourage children to write their own leaflets titled: 'What my pet needs' (a home, food, exercise and love).	animal feeds, containers, drinking bowls and other equipment such as dog leads.	different. Sort out the feeds and water containers. Match to the correct animal. Dog biscuits and cans of food are all different shapes and sizes.
4	Write lists of items you would need to care for your new pet. A dog would need food, water, bowls, collar, lead, name tag and a bed.	Sort and match food using shape, size and colour. Begin to weigh food and use non-standard units of weight and comparative language: lighter than, heavier than and the same as.	When you travel, can animals always go with you? What happens to pets then? Design carrying boxes for different toy animals.
5	Think of suitable pets for different people considering where they live. Act out an old man in a flat buying a pet, a little girl on a farm, a family wanting a pet and discuss in role which pet they choose and why.	Make a picture plan of where they are going to exercise their pet.	Take an animal on a journey and think about all the equipment you need to take with you.

Table 23   Zoo or safari park

Date	Role play	Shops: Zoo or safari park	
	Com./lang./lit. development	Mathematical development	Other areas of development
1	Discuss whether anyone has ever visited one. What did they do there? Who did they go with? How are they different from pet shops? What happened to them when they visited? Read *Zoo Hullabaloo* about the inside of a zoo. How	Describe the journey there. Sort and count the animals.	Set up the areas both indoors and outside. Use a white board for instant props. Use soft toys, masks of the animals and wear costumes for the workers. Look in books, ICT for information about each animal (notices on each

Table 23   *(Contd)*

Date	Role play	Shops: Zoo or safari park	
	Com./lang./lit. development	Mathematical development	Other areas of development
	could we set one up in class? Think of roles, animals, keepers, ticket office and visitors.		enclosure). These are often wild animals not pets.
2	Increase vocabulary by learning animals' names and information about their needs. Write notices, tickets and labels for the area. Think carefully about safety.	Count the animals in the enclosures and pens. Look at the different sizes of enclosures depending on which animal they are housing. Think about the cost of visiting and buying tickets using real money.	Make enclosures for the animals both inside and out using a variety of materials ensuring each one has a gate and a place for the animals to shelter under (boxes and construction kits). Consider their manners when buying tickets: please and thank you.
3	Act out a visit to a zoo or safari park with them playing a variety of roles including some of the animals.	Think about what the animals need to eat. Counting, weighing and measuring the amounts. Decide the order of giving the food to animals.	Draw plans of the zoo or safari park showing the road, paths, entrances and exits.
4	Read *Dear Zoo*. What do you think would happen if an animal got sick? Who would they need to telephone?	Decide the order of animals and make a rota for feeding. Make notices with opening times on.	Use the toy cars to move around the safari park outdoors. How do the keepers transport the food and animals around?
5	Create a problem: an animal escapes. Think whether they need any new props. Record their story by tape, photograph, pictures or writing for the class to share later.	Make posters with sets of animals on.	Discuss where these animals come from and look at maps or globes of the world. Think about what it is like there and how zoos try to recreate natural areas. Let the children begin to realise that there are very few of some species and that zoos and safari parks are trying to keep them safe.

TRANSPORT AND JOURNEYS

Road, rail and air

Play situation

Create a vehicle (train, bus, aeroplane, car, lorry, bicycle, rocket or spaceship) in which children can go to various imaginary destinations of their choice. It will comprise the vehicle, numbered or coded seats, doorway, driving seat, steering wheel, controls, engine, windows, mechanics and support services: a ticket controller either in an office or travel agent's, or a conductor on a bus. The children will be able to buy tickets for a chosen destination, get on the vehicle, store their baggage and pretend to travel. There are numerous roles for the children to play within this scenario: drivers, passengers, mechanics or office staff, and they will begin to understand the factors that affect people even if they only go on a short journey. (See Tables 24–28.)

> ## Introductory prompts
>
> Why do we need to travel?
> Where can I go to find out about travel?
> Have any of them ever been on a journey? Where did they go? How did they travel there?
> How do they travel to school?
> How do they know where the vehicle is going?
> Is the journey going to be long or short?
> Where can you get food from when you travel?
> What happens if the vehicle breaks down?

Possible roles

CAR OR LORRY OR BICYCLE: driver, rider, passengers, garage staff, mechanics, office staff, police and road safety personnel

TRAIN: train driver, guard, ticket collector, station ticket office person, cleaners, passengers and mechanics

BUS OR COACH: bus driver, passengers, bus conductor or officer selling tickets, mechanics, passengers and cleaners

AEROPLANE: pilot, flight crew, air steward and cabin crew, passengers, baggage controllers, checking and weighing-in staff, food controllers, arrivals officers, departure officers and mechanics

ROCKET OR SPACESHIP: space crew, astronauts, flight control, mechanics and scientists

Resources

Supply uniforms, hats, chairs, trolleys, luggage, tickets, brochures, timetables, office desk, writing tools, calendars, telephones, mobile phones, computer keyboard, VDU screen, stamper, money, tills, engine (construction kits), steering wheel, gear stick and pedals (construction kits), tools for mechanics, Brio and real tools, rolling white board for drawing props, control panel (batteries and bulbs), card, boxes, paint.
  See Recommended reading for books about road, rail and air transport.

Potential learning opportunities

Personal, social and emotional development

The road, rail and air transport role-play scenarios will help the children to:

Disposition and attitude

- explore a new learning environment involved with transport projects with imagination, creativity, confidence, humour and persistence;
- initiate play, building on their own experiences of travel; begin to take a lead in the play and organise others;
- discuss their own play journeys with peers and adults confidently;

Self-confidence and self-esteem

- improve their confidence and begin to develop and be proud of their own personality;

Making relationships/behaviour/self-control

- express feelings and be sensitive to the needs of others;
- work cooperatively within a small group, showing respect, interest and care for others;

107

Transport and journeys

- share the role-play resources and space, take turns fairly, form queues and be polite;
- explore the need for their own simple rules within the area for safety reasons;
- play independently within the role-play area: buying tickets, finding seats, dealing with baggage and enjoying the journey;

Self-care

- select appropriate equipment for a task and use it sensibly and feel confident to ask for advice and help from peers and supporting adults if problems arise or equipment is not available;
- improve their dressing skills by tackling various types of clothes and fastenings when wearing costumes;

Sense of community

- be aware of the different transport systems that operate in their own local area and further afield;
- understand how transport systems have changed with time.

Communication, language and literacy

The road, rail and air transport role-play scenarios will help the children to:

Speaking, listening and communicating

- speak clearly and use appropriate body language to get attention, defend their own interests and to be understood by friends and family;
- develop questioning techniques (how, when, where and why) about where vehicles are travelling, how much the journey costs and the times involved;
- begin to use language as a means of communicating: giving simple instructions, explaining routes and directions, asking for help, expressing opinions and responding to aural stimuli from telephones, passengers' requests, computers and other equipment;
- share with the group what they have achieved through play;

Reading and linking sounds to letters

- develop a need to read and awareness of environmental print: posters, leaflets, tickets, maps, brochures, magazines and timetables;
- listen with interest to and read a selection of stories and non-fiction books, magazines and other class-made reading material about relevant transport and travel topics;
- retell some of the stories using drama as a tool remembering the main characters, sequence of events and key rhymes and chants;
- create real life stories which can be recorded in a format that the children choose: video, photograph, tape, picture or writing;

Writing

- develop their confidence and enjoyment of being able to write by experimenting with mark-making tools in the role-play area and writing their own and their friends' names on play documents;
- write using emergent, symbolic and conventional letter forms, postcards from various destinations, posters, leaflets and other advertising material using travel brochures and magazines to develop them;
- make zig-zag books to capture different stages of the children's imaginary journey.

Mathematical development

The road, rail and air transport role-play scenarios will help the children to:

Representation

- record information about the number of travellers on a given journey in pictorial and numerical forms (Which were the most popular seats and why? Which was the most popular destination?);

Sorting/matching/ordering

- sort and match tools used by mechanics according to shape, size and colour and place them in appropriately labelled boxes and on shelves;
- match one seat on a vehicle to one child with a correctly numbered, coloured or shaped ticket;

Number

- recognise numerals in the environment: on signs, tickets, catalogues and travel brochures;
- recite numbers in the correct order up to ten and beyond by singing lots of number rhymes using forward and backward counting techniques;
- place number labels onto vehicle seats in the correct order;
- count reliably up to ten objects or people and begin to make sensible estimates of the number of people on a vehicle up to ten;
- recognise, name, handle and use money in the role-play scenarios for buying and selling transport tickets;
- exchange coins for the same value up to 5p when they buy and sell tickets;
- introduce the idea of ordinal numbers, (first, second etc.) and incorporate them into play: queues and arrivals etc.;

Calculations

- begin to use language such as more than, less than and the same as, about the number of passengers in play scenarios;

Transport and journeys

- solve practical problems involving counting in everyday situations on transport;
- add two sets of people together: the people in the green carriage and the blue carriage;
- add and subtract money in simple play situations;

Shape, space and measure

- discuss shapes and their properties relating to those of the props: windows, wheels and carriages;

Size/area/length

- discuss and measure the size, length and height of the vehicle;
- discuss an imaginary or real journey using positional and directional language;

Capacity/volume

- investigate capacity by filling, emptying and comparing containers for washing and cleaning the vehicles;
- explore ways of measuring capacity and developing the need for a standard measure, e.g. litre;

Time

- understand the times of the day: morning, lunch, afternoon, evening, night;
- identify the days of the week and months of the year;
- understand the importance of having watches and clocks to arrive at places on time;
- develop the skill of telling the time using o'clock;
- make a timetable giving times and journeys the vehicle is making.

Knowledge and understanding of the world

The road, rail and air transport role-play scenarios will help the children to:

Attitudes and interests

- show interest in gaining more information from non-fiction books, magazines, photographs and other evidence about transport issues and discuss them;

Observe, explore, investigate and classify

- group a selection of small transport toys according to observable attributes;
- make observational drawing, paintings and models of vehicles from real life, models or photographs;
- use small play models and investigate how the vehicles work: train and track, or a jet engine using a balloon;

Materials and their properties

- identify, sort and have an understanding of some of the properties of different materials and why they are used for different purposes in making vehicles;
- develop skills in using tools and materials and choose the relevant ones for a particular task, e.g. making an engine using scrap materials;

Environment

- understand how vehicles and people can affect the environment both locally and worldwide;
- discuss pollution and what may be done to reduce it;

Physical processes/light/sound

- understand that energy or force is involved in moving objects;
- gain an awareness of energy sources (petrol, wind etc.);
- investigate the forces of pushing and pulling toy vehicles and record what happens to them;
- investigate toys with mechanisms that make them move, e.g. motor, batteries or clockwork;
- investigate and know ways of making sounds and lights and use this knowledge to make safe lights and sounds for the role-play vehicle;

Weather and seasons

- consider the weather, season and time of day when making a journey and how these affect how and when a vehicle is used;

111

Transport and journeys

Design and making

- design and make props for the role-play area using a wide range of materials and tools. Visit an area of local interest, e.g. a bus station or railway station, to gain ideas;
- identify and name parts of the vehicle and support services having some idea of their function, e.g. wheels: movement, windows: view;

Sense of time and place

- extend their knowledge of transport using practical and dramatic approaches showing an understanding of why we need to travel;
- know why people need plans and maps and what they use them for;
- discuss a journey they have been on and the transport used;
- explore and investigate the history of vehicles and discover how they have changed with time (models, photographs and stories of real events);

ICT

- complement their learning using My World, Towns and Thomas the Clown CD-ROM (position and directions);
- use Roamer and other pre-programmed toys.

Creative development

The road, rail and air transport role-play scenarios will help the children to:

Exploring media and materials

- create observational work based on real life experiences: make posters and pictures giving information to decorate the role-play area;
- use a variety of tools and materials to create collages of workers and give them names and identities;
- make large-scale props out of card and boxes to support the role play;

Music

- listen to and join in with rhymes about transport: *Tom Thumb's Musical Maths*: 'Five wonky bicycles', 'Mary up in her spaceship', *Okki-tokki-unga*: 'Wheels on the Bus', *Apusskidu*: 'The train is a-coming', 'She'll be coming round the mountain', *Bingo lingo*: 'Little red jeep', 'Captain of the aeroplane'.
- use simple instruments to complement their singing: 'The Little Red Jeep', 'The Aliens'.
- listen to theme tunes from popular TV programmes, e.g. 'Thomas the Tank Engine'.

Imagination

- use drama to recreate what it is like to book and travel on a vehicle and the adventures that may happen;

- encourage the children to solve problems through dramatic play, e.g. breakdown or an object on the track;

Physical development

The road, rail and air transport role-play scenarios will help the children to:

Movements

- improve fine and gross motor movements using tools and equipment;
- use a wide range of materials when they construct or use vehicles to develop their coordination;
- observe how different vehicles move and imitate them;

Health and bodily awareness

- be aware of safety when travelling on vehicles;
- be aware of road, rail and air safety.

Talking points

Which vehicle did you enjoy travelling on?
Where did you go?
How long did it take?
How much money did it cost?
Did you travel alone or with a friend?
Have you been on any vehicles with your parents?
Do vehicles have any entertainment on board?
Can you buy food while travelling?
Could you sleep?
How many passengers were on the vehicle?
Who looked after them?
Where did their luggage go?
How could they identify it?

Key vocabulary

BUS OR COACH: Bus, coach, bus stop, bus/coach station, wheels, door, windows, upstairs, downstairs, bell, wipers, lights, seats, aisle, steering wheel, breaks, driver, passenger, money, ticket, ticket machine, queue, ordinal numbers, luggage rack

TRAIN: Train, engine, carriages, diesel, steam engine, controls, passengers, driver, guard, ticket officer, information officer, food staff on and off train, uniforms, rails, track, signal, platform, station, telephone, writing tools, tickets, ticket inspector, fast, slow

AEROPLANE: Aeroplane, helicopter, jet, pilot, flight attendants, ground control, mechanic, tools, uniforms, cockpit, controls, lights, dials, windows, wings, propeller, take off, landing, seats, seat belts, headrest, toilet, door, passengers, luggage, passports, TV, radio, magazines, brochures, food, timetable, emergency

ROCKET OR SPACESHIP: Rocket, spaceship, control, astronauts, mission control, radar people, stars, planets, tools, moon boots, buggy, repair manual, fuel tanks, air tanks, headphones, flag, radio, first aid kit, maps, charts, computer, lift off

Observational focus

Observe and ask the children to show you how we use different modes of transport.

1. Cannot remember any significant information/detail ☐
2. Can remember a small amount of information and detail ☐
3. Can give a full account of how to use different modes of transport ☐
4. Can extend play and create new characters and scenarios ☐

Table 24 Bus or coach

Date	Role play	Transport: Bus or coach	
	Com./lang./lit. development	Mathematical development	Other areas of development
1	Discuss setting up an area as a bus and a bus station. Let the children think which props they will need, rules that apply when they play, number of children and roles to be played: bus driver, passengers, bus conductor and inspector. Where do you go to catch a bus?	Use shape, colour and texture to create a new area. Think about the size and shape of windows and doors. Think about the wheels: what would happen if they were square? Decide on the number of seats the bus will have. Count people on and off the bus. Have five children to begin with and work up to ten. Try and predict how many are left etc.	Make simple props, card with holes for windows or with children's pictures drawn on a revolving white board which change when appropriate. Talk about and make a bell for the passengers to stop the bus when they need to get off. Construct the engine and steering wheel using construction and boxes.
2	Talk about a real bus journey they have been on with their family or friends. Read posters and leaflets advertising	Give the bus a number (changeable) and decide where it is going: to the shops, school run, sports centre etc. Introduce	Make some bus stops and allow places for people to queue. Deal sensibly with shopping and other baggage. Help

Table 24 *(Contd)*

Date	Role play	Transport: Bus or coach	
	Com./lang./lit. development	Mathematical development	Other areas of development
	where to go. Discuss the advantages of using a bus over a car. Read *The Big Red Bus*.	ordinal numbers using real people who wait in a queue.	mums on to the bus with buggies. Have mechanics with tools checking the engine when it comes back to the bus station.
3	While waiting for a bus the children can talk in character (informally). Start making tickets and writing bus numbers on each one. Make posters for the bus station giving passengers instructions and information.	Discuss how much the tickets will cost. Write the price on tickets. Recognise and use money for fares. Will there be more than one price? Will we have passes for elderly people? Start to issue them when the correct money has been paid.	The importance of polite social behaviour when they talk and work with people. Respect what others say and listen carefully to them. Make room for elderly or disabled people to sit down.
4	Discuss an imaginary journey where the children decide what happens. Draw pictures of your imaginary journey. What will they need for a day trip (packed lunch, coats and umbrella)?	Discuss positional language used for seating: opposite, under, behind, next to, left, right (use arrows). Talk about sitting and standing. Think about upstairs and downstairs. Discuss route of journey.	Think of a problem: the bus breaks down, they are on the wrong bus or they have no money. The children have to work through a scenario taking their own twists and turns.
5	Children play with peers queueing and interacting with each other. Children can sequence their role play into a story that can be shared with others. Learn and sing 'The Wheels on the Bus' with actions. Make up new verses, add instruments and tape it.	The children look at the times a bus is due on a simple timetable (on the hour) and use the vocabulary for the days of the week.	Discuss reasons for fixtures on bus (mechanics). What are they used for: wheels, electronic door and bell. The children must be made aware of the danger when getting on and off the bus and while the bus is moving.

Table 25 Aeroplane

Date	Role play	Transport: Aeroplane	
	Com./lang./lit. development	Mathematical development	Other areas of development
1	Find out who has flown. Get them to share experiences. Decide which props and roles are needed: pilot, air crew, ground crew, and areas they need to make an airport: aeroplanes, terminal buildings and runways. Use non-fiction books to help. Gather hats and costumes together.	Make windows for plane with views (rolling white board). Put in numbered seats in twos and threes and put on the correct number of seat belts. Make a simple cockpit with seat, joystick and controls painted on.	Think about the types of machines that fly: aeroplanes, hang-gliders, helicopters, balloons, rockets and spaceships. Some air transport needs fuel to make it move. Sing 'Captain of the Aeroplane'.
2	Make posters and information booklets using travel brochures. Read stories about flying: *Topsy and Tim* or *My First Flight*. Make activities for children to do on a flight. Discuss people in story.	Make tickets to match seats. Encourage the children to use real money to buy and sell them. Look at the luggage people take with them. Label it with children's names and check it in, give it a special hold number.	Use PE mats to make a runway with warning lights. Reinforce safety when flying: wearing seatbelts, parachutes and listening carefully to instructions given by the flight crew.
3	Discuss where they may travel to and why. What do they need to take with them? Make passports with photographs on.	Think about the distances travelled (near or far) and the time spent in the air.	Think of the people who work on the ground (mechanics) and fix the planes. Collect tools and equipment for them.
4	Take on roles and pretend to go on holiday. What do they have to do in an airport? Book in, check your luggage, get boarding passes, wait for your flight to be called, show passport, board, take off, flight (flight crew looking after you and pilot telling you about journey) and landing with adult support.	Design a menu for the flight. Make the correct number of meals for passengers out of dough and other materials. What food would be suitable?	Encourage the children to take on roles of cleaning staff and keep the plane tidy and clean.

Table 25 *(Contd)*

Date	Role play	Transport: Aeroplane	
	Com./lang./lit. development	Mathematical development	Other areas of development
5	Think of scenarios where an emergency could happen. Encourage the children to play independently in area developing it to suit their needs.	Discuss directions and practise them outdoors or in a large open space.	Discuss the importance of knowing what the weather forecasts are.

Table 26 Space travel

Date	Role play	Travel: Rocket and space travel	
	Com./lang./lit. development	Mathematical development	Other areas of development
1	Read *Whatever Next*. Discuss and collect materials together to act out the story using their imagination. The children work in small groups to think of ways they may extend or modify the story.	Read *Countdown* (with flaps). Make and count stars and planets as you travel. Sing 'The rocket number song'.	Look in non-fiction books and find out about space travel. Look at the crafts and rockets used.
2	Think about the people who launch and fly real rockets (astronaut, scientists, mechanics and ground support staff). Equipment and props they would need (tools, fuel, radio system with microphone, space food). What clothes do they need (spacesuit, moon boots and air tanks)?	Make a control panel. Discuss which buttons to press to take off, land and other important jobs.	The children start to make a rocket or spaceship using boxes and other materials. Start to develop the space terminal with maps, charts, radio, telephone, computer and writing materials.
3	Start a scenario where the rocket takes off into space. Have all the children in role and start to count down. Communicate	Use moon buggy (bike) to move around the planet. Make a moon surface using 2-D and 3-D shapes. Take routes around them discussing	Investigate the idea of no air or gravity in space and items just floating about. Use a large space and move freely while they

117

Table 26 *(Contd)*

Date	Role play	Travel: Rocket and space travel	
	Com./lang./lit. development	Mathematical development	Other areas of development
	with ground control using radio. Record what happens in pictures in a class space book. Use photographs to illustrate it.	direction, speed and position. Think about directions and time (air supply).	consider gravity.
4	Read stories and watch films about fantasy space travel and aliens (*Meg and Mog on the Moon, Dinosaurs* and *All That Rubbish*).	Learn some space number rhymes: 'Five little men in a flying saucer'.	Create a fantasy spaceship, think about its shape, windows, controls and the materials that it is made of.
5	Create a space story orally. Who do they meet in space? Describe and draw them. What are they doing? Do they like you being there? What do they do next? Where do they go? How does it all end? Use tapes to record different space stories.	Sort and match large planets and stars using colour and shape as criteria.	Pretend to be aliens using props, sounds and movements. Try to create stories around them related to spaceships and rockets. Make large pictures of aliens and space monsters to illustrate your tales.

Table 27 Train

Date	Role play	Transport: Train	
	Com./lang./lit. development	Mathematical development	Other areas of development
1	Discuss setting up the area as a train and station and what props they will need, rules that apply when playing, number of children and roles to be played: train driver, passengers, ticket seller, guard, inspector, track walkers and mechanics. Discuss	Use rectangular mats to represent carriages. Make windows and doors and think about their shape with different views out of them. Put numbers on the seats in the train.	Make simple props: card with holes for windows or with children's pictures drawn on a revolving white board, which change when appropriate. Introduce a whistle for the guard to stop the train to let passengers on and off. Let the children construct a simple

Table 27 *(Contd)*

Date	Role play	Transport: Train	
	Com./lang./lit. development	Mathematical development	Other areas of development
	how they catch a train.		engine and steering wheel using construction and boxes.
2	Read *The Train Ride* and discuss what the children see. Read posters that tell of journeys they can take on trains. Discuss why train travel is enjoyable. Use a microphone to tell passengers which train to get on, where it is going and times.	Give the train a number (changeable) and decide where it is going. Think about how trains often travel long distances. Begin to use ordinal numbers referring to real people waiting in a queue or carriages.	Develop a station with a platform, office and railway line. Deal with shopping and other baggage in the guard's van.
3	Start making train-shaped tickets with seat numbers on and prices. Have a selection of Thomas the Tank Engine books available for the children to read freely.	Discuss how much the tickets will cost. Put the price on tickets. Will there be more than one price? Will we have rail passes for people with photographs? Start to issue them when the correct money has been paid.	Importance of polite behaviour when talking and working with people. Respect what others say and listen carefully to them. Make room for elderly or disabled people to sit down.
4	Discuss an imaginary journey and let the children decide what happens. Draw pictures of things you see on your imaginary journey.	Discuss positional language using: at the front and at the back. Who is sitting where? Talk about people sitting and standing. Which carriages are they in: first or second?	Find out about how trains have changed (non-fiction books). Make the children aware of the danger of playing on or near railways and how it is against the law.
5	Develop the idea of a journey into a picture map with photographs and children's pictures along a railway line on a large sheet of paper.	Counting people getting on and off the train. Start with five children to and work up to ten. Try and predict how many are left.	Think of a problem: getting on the wrong express train or objects on the line, and get the children to work through the scenario with its own twists and turns. Stress the importance of safety in all play.

Table 28   Cars and garage

Date	Role play	Transport: Cars and garage	
	Com./lang./lit. development	Mathematical development	Other areas of development
1	We use cars, lorries and bikes on the roads. What do we need in the garage (tools, ramps, lights, wheels, parts, fuel and pumps, paints, office till, computer, writing materials, order book and vehicle-shaped report cards)?	Sort vehicles according to the number of wheels they have. Sort them again according to the job they do.	Different types of traffic on the roads: why is it different and what is it used for? Read *The Little Blue Car*. Collect pictures from car manufacturers and magazines.
2	The children describe a road vehicle that they know. What is its colour, make and size? How many passengers will it hold? Draw or paint a picture of it. Make road signs for Stop, Go and road works, to use outside.	Look at the shapes of road signs and sort them. Design own signs for playground roads. Make a book showing shaped environmental signs. What sign can you see?	Discuss safety: seat belts, road safety using cars outside, looking out for traffic lights, crossings and road works.
3	Set up a simple garage with two mechanics (overalls and gloves). Discuss jobs that go on there. In the office have an order book for jobs. Book in vehicles and make appropriate report cards. Develop vocabulary with parts of vehicles: wheels, door, windscreen, boot, bonnet, exhaust, steering wheel, brake, engine etc. Develop characters and give them names.	Match, count and record nuts and bolts used in garage. Investigate fuel in the water tray by pouring into small holed containers. Use pipes and funnels to help. Think about capacity. Set up a simple car wash outside with hoses, sprays, buckets, sponges and detergents. Buy fuel from garage forecourt from a pump and pay in the kiosk.	Make props for garage: ramps, petrol pumps, tool trays (shadow). Make engines and other vehicle parts using construction kits.
4	Discuss an imaginary journey where the children decide what happens. Draw pictures of your imaginary journey: go on holiday,	Find a space and park in a car park. Make car and bike-shaped tickets. Put money into a machine or give to a person and find a numbered parking	The importance of polite behaviour when talking and working with people. Respect what others say and listen carefully to them.

120

Table 28 *(Contd)*

Date	Role play	Transport: Cars and garage	
	Com./lang./lit. development	Mathematical development	Other areas of development
	have an adventure, go to the shops or visit someone special.	spot outside with big bikes and cars. Manoeuvre the vehicles into position and remember to display ticket and lock up.	
5	Look at emergency vehicles. Where do they come from? How are they contacted? The children set up a scenario using one or more emergency vehicle. They could be reporters who discuss a situation while it happens: an accident on the road, fire or someone trapped. Make posters about keeping safe on the roads.	Children use telephones to contact emergency services using 999. Think about directions and how to describe them.	Use remote control cars and racing car sets. Turn Roamer into a vehicle of their choice and program it to go on a journey.

Boats and water

Play situation

Create an area in which children can go and explore different aspects of water and boats. It will comprise a variety of small and large boats surrounded by a pretend watery environment. The boats will need a driving seat, steering wheel, controls, engine, sails, paddles, windows, portholes and support services, a ticket controller either in an office or on board, travel agents, mechanics and engineers. The children will buy tickets for a chosen destination, get on the boat where any baggage will be dealt with, and pretend to travel there. There are numerous roles for the children to play within this scenario: drivers, passengers, mechanics and office staff, and they will begin to understand the factors that affect people even if they only go on a short journey. Real and imaginary objects, displays and the water tray will be used to create the watery environment and set up an area for an aquarium. (See Table 29.)

Introductory prompts

Has anyone ever been in a boat?
What did it feel like?
What sort of boat was it?
Where did they go?
Why do we need to travel?
Where can I go to find out about travel?
Is the journey going to be long or short?
Where can they get food from?
What happens when the boat breaks down?
How do they know where the boat is going?
Where does water come from?
Do any creatures live in water?
Do any plants live in water?
How could we find out about them?
Has anyone ever seen underwater? Where?

Possible roles

BOAT: captain, sailors, crew, passengers, luggage controllers, restaurant staff, recreational facilities staff, entertainment staff, cleaner and mechanics

WATERY ENVIRONMENT: fish and other creatures, fishermen, divers, aquarium staff, wildlife experts and presenters

Resources

Provide uniforms, hats, chairs, trolleys, luggage, tickets, brochures, timetables, office desk, writing tools, calendars, telephones, mobile phones, computer keyboard, VDU screen, stamper, money, tills, engine (construction), steering wheel, gear stick, tools for mechanics (Brio and real tools), rolling white board (draw props), card, boxes, paint, diving gear, flippers, masks, paintings, models of underwater worlds, pretend underwater creatures and plants, shipwreck, treasure. Perhaps use a paddling pool and seaside equipment.
See Recommended reading for books about boats and water.

Link activities

Make models, pictures and collages of workers and boats and give them names.
Devise a simple test to investigate how boats are powered.
Make observation works of underwater creatures and plants.
Discuss what the creatures eat.
Visit harbours, ferry ports and docks if possible and discuss what they see.
Think about pollution and how we can keep water clean.
Stress the importance of safety around water.

Potential learning opportunities

Personal, social and emotional development

The boats and water role-play scenarios will help the children to:

Disposition and attitude

- explore a new learning environment with imagination, creativity, confidence, humour and persistence;
- initiate play and build on their own experiences of travel and begin to take a lead in the play and organise others;
- discuss their own play boat journeys with peers and adults confidently;
- develop an understanding and care for other living things;

Self-confidence and self-esteem

- improve their own confidence and begin to develop their own personal character and personality;
- feel confident to ask for advice and help from peers and supporting adults;

Making relationships/behaviour/self-control

- express their feelings and be sensitive to the needs of others;
- develop relationships with other children showing respect, interest and care for others;
- form queues, take turns fairly and be polite to each other and supporting adults;
- share the role-play resources and space fairly so that their play can develop, they can take turns, develop self-made rules of behaviour and improve their ability to work as a member of a group;
- play independently within the area by being able to buy tickets, find seats, deal with baggage and enjoy a journey or investigate an underwater world;

Self-care

- be aware of their own personal needs, be able to ask for assistance, tackle new problems confidently, e.g. dressing, using equipment, and to be proud of their own achievements;

Sense of community

- explore and investigate whether water has any part in their daily lives or that of the community they live in.

Communication, language and literacy

The boats and water role-play scenarios will help the children to:

123

Speaking, listening and communicating

- speak clearly and use appropriate body language to get attention, to defend their own interests and to be understood by friends while playing;
- respond to aural stimuli: the telephone, passengers' requests, information from computers and other equipment;
- develop questioning techniques: how, when, where and why, related to where boats are going, how much the journey costs and the times involved;
- begin to use language as a means of communicating to give simple instructions, ask for help and express opinions;
- share with the group what they have achieved through their play;
- give guided tours around the aquarium or wildlife boat trips, perhaps with glass bottoms, using specific descriptive language;

Reading and linking sounds to letters

- listen to with interest and read a selection of fiction and non-fiction books, magazines and other reading material about relevant boat travel and underwater life;
- retell some of the stories using drama as a tool, remembering the main characters, sequence of events and key rhymes and chants;
- create real life stories which can be recorded in a format the children choose, e.g. video, photograph, tape, picture or writing;
- develop an awareness of environmental print: posters, leaflets, tickets, magazines and timetables for boats and the aquarium;

Writing

- develop their confidence and write using a wide variety of mark-making tools: their names and familiar words on posters, leaflets, signs for aquarium, postcards, receipts, tickets and other advertising material using travel brochures and magazines in the role-play area;
- make a range of books capturing different stages of the children's real or imaginary journey showing who they meet or give a pictorial account (log) of their journey.

Mathematical development

The boats and water role-play scenarios will help the children to:

Representation

- record information about the number of travellers on a given journey or the number of sea creatures found in a variety of forms. (Which were the most popular seats and why? Which was the most popular destination?);

Sorting/matching/ordering

- sort and match boats, tools, water creatures and plants according to shape, size, colour and function;

- match one seat on the boat to one child with the correct ticket, or the correct food to a sea creature;
- sort and match coins and tickets;
- sort and match creatures to different tanks in the aquarium using labels;

Number

- recognise numerals in the environment: on signs, tickets, catalogues or travel brochures;
- recite numbers in the correct order up to ten and sing lots of number rhymes using forward and backward counting techniques;
- place number labels onto boat seats and tickets seats in the correct order;
- count reliably up to ten objects: people, fish caught or creatures in the aquarium, and begin to make sensible estimates up to ten;
- recognise, name, handle and use money in the role-play scenarios to buy and sell boat or aquarium tickets;
- introduce the idea of ordinal numbers: first, second etc. and incorporate them into play, e.g. queues, arrivals;

Calculations

- begin to use language such as more than, less than and the same, in the play scenarios;
- solve practical problems involving counting in everyday situations by adding two sets of people or underwater creatures together;
- add and subtract money in simple play situations;

Shape, space and measure

- discuss shapes and their properties regarding role-play props: boats, portholes or air tanks;

Size/area/length

- discuss and measure the size, length and height of the boats and underwater creatures;
- discuss a real or imaginary journey using positional and directional language;

Capacity/volume

- investigate capacity by filling, emptying and comparing containers for transporting water on a journey and begin to introduce non-standard measures;

Time

- understand the times of the day: morning, lunch, afternoon, evening and night;
- identify the days of the week and months of the year;

- understand the importance of having watches and clocks to arrive at places on time;
- develop the skill of telling the time using o'clock;
- make a timetable giving times and journeys the boat is making, or feeding times at the aquarium.

Knowledge and understanding of the world

The boats and water role-play scenarios will help the children to:

Attitudes and interests

- show interest and begin to gain more information from non-fiction books and photographs and talk about them;

Observe, explore, investigate and classify

- group a selection of small boats or underwater creatures according to observable attributes;
- make observational drawing, paintings or models of boats and underwater creatures from real life or photographs using a wide range of materials;
- use small play models to investigate how boats float;

Materials and their properties

- begin to identify, sort and have an understanding of some of the properties of different materials and why they are used for different purposes, e.g. sort a variety of everyday objects using sinking and floating as criteria;
- think about the materials used in making boats and try them out;
- develop skills using tools and materials, and choose the relevant ones for a task, e.g. to make a selection of differently powered boats using scrap materials;

Life processes and living things

- distinguish between living creatures and plants and non-living things;
- be aware of the needs and characteristics (discuss their differences and similarities) of underwater creatures and plants and show them care and consideration;
- visit a local pet shop that stocks tropical fish and identify the equipment needed to care for them;

Environment

- understand how boats and people can affect the environment both locally and worldwide;
- discuss pollution and what may be done to reduce it;

Physical processes/light/sound

- understand that energy or force are involved in moving objects;
- be aware of energy sources: petrol, wind etc;
- investigate the forces of pushing and pulling with toy vehicles and record what happens to them in pictorial form;
- investigate boats with mechanisms that make them move, e.g. motor, batteries, clockwork, and have some understanding of how they work;
- investigate ways of making sounds and lights and incorporate them safely on to the role-play boats;
- discuss how the weather and seasons change and how this may affect journeys;

Design and making

- design and make props for the role-play area using a wide range of materials and tools. Visit areas of local interest, e.g. ferry ports, harbours, boatyards, canals and aquariums to gain new ideas;
- identify and name parts of a boat having some idea of their make-up and function, e.g. portholes/view, wheel/steering, paddle/power;
- make boats out of different materials, test them and record the results;

Sense of time and place

- understand why we need to travel using boats and the importance of plans and maps when planning a journey;
- discuss an imaginary or real journey on water and the transport used;
- explore and investigate historical sources connected to boats and discover how they have changed with time (models, photographs and stories of real events);

ICT

- use Roamer and other pre-programmed toys: remote controlled boats.

Creative development

The boats and water role-play scenarios will help the children to:

Exploring media and materials

- create observational work based on real life experiences and make posters and pictures giving information to decorate the role-play area (boats, people, underwater creatures and plants, shipwrecks);
- use a variety of tools and materials to create collages of workers (on boats, in aquarium, wildlife presenters and experts) and give them names;
- make simple large-scale props out of card, boxes etc. (box boat) to support the role play;
- make boats using different materials and techniques: paper folding, junk models and dough, testing their effectiveness;

Music

- listen to and join in with rhymes and songs about water life and boats: *Appuskidu*, 'Yellow submarine', 'My ship sailed from China', *Silver Burdett*, 'A sailor went to sea', 'Weather sound effects: Rain drops'; *Okki-toki-unga*, 'Row row your boat', 'The big ship sails on the Alley Alley Oh';
- use simple instruments to complement their singing;
- listen to a range of watery music: 'Octopus's garden' by the Beatles, 'The Aquarium' from *Carnival of the Animals*;

Imagination

- use role play to take on new roles and to recreate what it is like to book and travel on a boat and the adventures that may happen;
- imagine what it must be like to live under the sea and take on the role of a diver to explore underwater worlds, perhaps finding a shipwreck with treasure;
- encourage the children to solve problems through dramatic play, e.g. breakdown, hole in boat or a sick underwater creature.

Physical development

The boat and water role-play scenarios will help the children to:

Movements

- improve fine motor control by using tools to construct the area and make individual boats and creative work;
- use a wide range of materials to develop coordination: to catch pretend fish;
- observe how different boats and underwater creatures move and imitate them, improving gross motor skills;
- visit a swimming pool to gain confidence in the water and start to learn how to swim;
- move freely to watery music;

Health and bodily awareness

- be aware of safety when travelling on boats and being around water.

Talking points

What sort of boat would you like to travel on? Why?
How fast does it go?
How many people fit on it?
Where would you like to go?
How much will it cost?

How do you know where to sit?
What happens on your journey?
Who do you see?
What do you find?
What happens to them?
Where could you go to see underwater creatures?
Can you keep them at home? How?

Key vocabulary

BOATS: Boat, sail, rowing, steam, canoe, ferry, liner, water, sink, float, depth, ripples, surf, anchor, tank, piston, pier, terminal, sailor, crew, captain, engineer, mechanics, uniforms, decks, portholes, hull, hatch, voyage, sea, river, waves, seaweed, fish, cargo, starboard, port, bow, stern, stowaway, weather, calm, wind, storm, rain, lightening and thunder.

UNDERWATER WORLD: Fish, sharks, eels, crabs, octopus, starfish, whales, dolphins, seals, water birds, seals, divers, wet suits, flippers, air tanks, masks, aquarium, tanks, food, health, attendant, guide, presenter, wildlife expert

Observational focus

Observe and ask the children to show you around the two areas: underwater and boats.

1. Cannot remember any significant information/detail □
2. Can remember a small amount of information/detail □
3. Can give a full account of boats and life underwater □
4. Can extend the play by creating new characters and scenarios □

Table 29   Boats and water

Date	Role play	Transport: Boats and water	
	Com./lang./lit. development	Mathematical development	Other areas of development
1	Read stories and poems about boats. Discuss if anyone has seen a boat or been on one. Did they enjoy it? What was the boat like? Describe it. Think of different kinds of boats. What sort of people work on or use	Have a variety of different-sized boxes for the children to make into pretend boats: rowing, sailing, submarine, motor boat. Decide how they are powered (row, sail, motor) and decorated. Decide how many people will fit in.	Investigate different types of boats using books, ICT, songs, rhymes and stories. If you live near any water or boats let the children visit and discuss what jobs the boats do. Think about safety on and around water (lifebuoys

Table 29   *(Contd)*

Date	Role play	Transport: Boats and water	
	Com./lang./lit. development	Mathematical development	Other areas of development
	them? What roles could the children take on?	Discuss and sort boats using the children's own criteria.	and life jackets).
2	Introduce the characters needed for the role play and give them identities depending on the size and type of boat. Read *Row Row Your Boat* and make simple props to help sequence the story. Let the children visit places that are of interest to them.	Record how the little boats (paper or junk) perform in a race. Introduce ordinal numbers.	Let the children sort a group of objects into those that float and those that sink. Make small boats out of a variety of materials to continue work on floating and sinking.
3	Think about boats that move large numbers of people around: ferries and cruise ships. How are they different from little boats? What can we find out about them? Make booklets using travel brochures. Design boat-shaped tickets for passengers with names and numbers on.	Use coloured mats to represent different areas on the ship. Describe the position of areas and how to get to them. What is the cost of different activities and food on board? Think about the cost of tickets depending on the type of ship and where you are travelling to.	Make large boats out of a variety of materials and put different numbers of play people in them and observe what happens to the boats. Think about submarines and how they stay under the water. Sing 'Yellow submarine'.
4	Look at pictures and videos of ferries and use positional language to describe what you see. Use this in role play as you are directing traffic on and off the ferry.	Look at photographs, adverts and videos of car ferries. Use an outdoor area and let the children drive the wheeled toys onto the ferry (mats with large construction and boxes to make ferry). Give tickets for each car giving it a specific position. Count the cars on and off. Look at the queues and the position of different cars.	Set up office and ticket booking area with telephones, writing materials etc. In the water tray make toy ferries for toy cars and people. Sing 'The big ship sails on the Alley Alley Oh'.

Table 29 *(Contd)*

Date	Role play	Transport: Boats and water	
	Com./lang./lit. development	Mathematical development	Other areas of development
5	Think about boats being used to fish or carry loads long distances, e.g. oil tankers, on the sea, lakes, rivers and canals. What roles and equipment would be needed on your boat and the docks? Sing 'My ship sails for China'.	Make a simple container ship for role play (large box or boxes with the sides cut away), fit other boxes (containers) or loads in. Think about shape, size and weight of cargo. How is it moved (cranes and machinery)?	Try loading toy boats in the water tray and recording how much they can carry before they sink.
6	Discuss what lives under the water. Read *Commotion in the Ocean* in small groups allowing the children to absorb the language and the illustrations. Watch an underwater video showing creatures and diving.	Use the water tray and a selection of small underwater creatures and sort into pairs. Sort using the children's own criteria.	Investigate life under water using books, videos and ICT (*My World: Fish Tank*). Paint pictures and make models of the creatures. Begin to develop an aquarium and discuss pollution. Make signs for aquarium.
7	Have guides taking people around telling others about the different creatures, needs and how it is important to care for all living things (aquarium).	Compare the number of creatures in different tanks. Use 'more' and 'less than' to compare them. Begin to add sets of creatures together to find the totals.	Discover what different creatures require to stay healthy in captivity and in the wild.
8	Let the children put on diving equipment. Talk about how we breathe under the water using air tanks. Pretend to dive and swim around underwater.	Record all the fascinating things you find. Count them.	Look at people who work with wildlife to try and keep it safe.
9	Encourage the children to imagine they have met a mermaid or fantasy creature who lives in the sea. Let the children give them a	Sort a selection of seashells in the water tray. Observe how they change colour when they dry off.	Paint large pictures of the creature or using lots of different materials.

131

Table 29 *(Contd)*

Date	Role play	Transport: Boats and water	
	Com./lang./lit. development	Mathematical development	Other areas of development
	name and bring the character to life.		
10	Imagine when diving they find an old shipwreck. Let them decide if they should explore. Think about the dangers and the excitement. What do they find (treasure, skeletons etc.)?	Think about how deep the water may have been. Can they think of ways to measure the depth of water?	Use an old box and create an old shipwreck. Look at videos and books to find out what they look like. Think about the seaweed which may have grown over it.
11	Discuss an adventure at sea: storms, icebergs, hole in boat, someone overboard. Develop the story into a short scenario with a beginning, middle and end.	Record the weather on charts measuring the amount of rain, sunshine and wind.	Use video cameras and photographs to record the children's play. Let the children share the recordings and encourage them to think of ways they could have developed their stories.

FAMILIAR STORIES

The Three Bears

Play situation

Create a play situation in the house corner where the story of Goldilocks and the Three Bears can be recreated and extended. There could be an outside area to act as the woodland. The cottage comprises all the usual house items but in threes: cups, plates, dishes, cutlery, chairs, beds etc. There are costumes and masks that the children can wear to help them get into role. (See Table 30.)

Introductory prompts

Do any of the children know the story?
Where have they heard it?
Has anyone ever seen real bears?
Where did you see them?
Could you stroke them? Why?
Could bears live in a cottage?
Do you think Goldilocks was a polite little girl?

Possible roles

Mummy Bear, Daddy Bear, Baby Bear, Goldilocks, Mum

Resources

Provide the three bears' cottage with furniture, cooking equipment, tea sets, dressing-up clothes, telephones, hairdryers, vacuum cleaner, cleaning equipment, place mats, irons and ironing boards, dolls of different kinds, masks and costumes. Have large pictures (child drawn) of trees, woodland, cottage etc.

Communication, literacy and language: books, magazines, labels, diaries, directories, notice board, message pads, shopping list booklets, notebooks, writing tools, telephones, pretend TV, tape recorder and radio.

Mathematical equipment: household items with numbers such as cookers, telephones, clocks, computers, videos, magazines, catalogues etc. which all use numbers for a variety of functions (price, time, distance, identification). A selection of items in sets of three which can be matched and sorted depending on a variety of criteria: colour, size, type and pattern.

A group of three objects that can be used to explore the concepts of position: cups, saucers, spoons, knives, forks, soft toys, dolls, large toys.

See Recommended reading for books about bears.

Link activities

Discuss when, why and how we wash our hands; sequence of the activity. Use a variety of soaps, brushes and creams.

Children bring in their pyjamas and pretend to go to bed and wake up, emphasising the importance of sleep.

Look at the sequence of dressing and undressing, using fastenings and turning clothes from being inside out, using bears as well as themselves.

Cook porridge and compare it to other cereals the children eat.

Have a teddy bears' tea party, sorting children's teddies, getting food ready, playing games and singing teddy songs.

Potential learning opportunities

Personal, social and emotional development

The Three Bears role play will help the children to:

Disposition and attitudes

- explore a new learning experience in the familiar setting of the home corner gradually changing it to the Three Bears' house;
- initiate play and build upon their knowledge of the story, their own experiences and ideas to solve and tackle new problems;

Self-confidence and self-esteem

- improve their confidence and begin to develop their own personal character and personality;
- develop an awareness of their own personal needs through the roles played and reflect and chat about their play to their peers and adults;
- bring their own teddies into school for a party and look after them;

Making relationships/behaviour/self-control

- through imaginative play express feelings and be sensitive to the needs of themselves and others;

- share the limited space fairly, take turns so that the play can expand, develop self-made rules of behaviour and improve their ability to work as a member of a group;

Self-care

- reinforce personal hygiene when eating and cooking;
- develop appropriate social skills for eating together: table manners, clearing away, washing up and tidying up;

Communication, language and literacy

The Three Bears role play will help the children to:

Speaking, listening and communicating

- speak clearly and use appropriate body language to get attention, defend their own interests and to be understood by friends and supporting adults;
- name everyday objects around the house, develop their language skills using adjectives to describe them, and put them into simple sentences;
- develop their questioning techniques: use simple instructions, ask for help and express opinions: I like or I dislike eating porridge;
- listen carefully to what others say when giving instructions and respond appropriately;
- use their language skills to take on and recreate familiar roles in the story;
- respond to and use appropriate social conventions such as please and thank you;

Reading

- listen to different versions of a traditional story: The Three Bears;
- retell the story and tape it and listen to each other;
- develop a sense of story sequence and the characters that make up the story;
- use real objects, puppets and sequence cards to retell it;
- read a selection of other bear stories to the children and compare the characters of the bears;
- be aware of environmental print and understand it carries meaning. Read the instructions for making porridge;
- read back their own writing in character;

Writing

- write a class book or little individual zig-zag books to retell the story and read them to each other;
- use household equipment and become familiar with how it works: cooker and microwave;
- know that words have meaning and develop their own need to be able to read and write;
- write in diaries, on forms and letters in character;
- make and write invitations for their teddies to come to a party at school.

Mathematical development

The Three Bears role play will help the children to:

Matching and sorting

- sort real objects within the Bears' house according to size, shape and other criteria;
- put toys away in appropriately labelled places and match objects using one-to-one correspondence: one spoon to one bowl;
- sort objects according to two criteria: small red cups, or function: something red to drink out of;
- sort and compare bears and children's own teddies using a variety of criteria;
- match one to one: teddy to one sweet or biscuit;
- match, recognise and write numbers around the Bear's home on cookers, videos, catalogues;

Size

- match objects to bears depending on their size (sing 'Goldilocks' Tale');
- order three objects and make sets of three big objects or three small objects;
- use language related to size: big, little, long, short, and introduce the tools used for measuring height;

Number

- count objects around the house developing an ability to estimate;
- recognise numbers up to ten and use them;
- investigate simple practical calculations involving addition and taking away;
- record whether they enjoyed the porridge or not and make a graph of the finding;

Shape/space and measure

- find different 2-D and 3-D shapes in the house and the environment and discuss their properties;

Length/weight/capacity/volume

- begin to use the language of weight and quantity when making the porridge;

Time

- discuss different times of the day and observe when different household activities occur: meals, bedtime and showers;
- begin to sequence events like cooking;
- use the names for the days of the week and times on the clock.

Knowledge and understanding of the world

The Three Bears role play will help the children to:

Living processes/living things/environment

- develop an awareness of some of the characteristics and needs of living things (bears);

Materials and their properties

- explore the differences between hot and cold and be aware of the dangers involved when cooking. Observe and record how materials change when heated: porridge before and after cooking;

Physical processes

- discuss some household appliances that use electricity and be aware of the dangers;

Sense of time

- look at old bears and old kitchen equipment and be aware of how things have changed over time;

Sense of place/ICT

- develop a sense of place by creating a map of Goldilocks' journey through the woods and around the house. Use Roamer to develop an awareness of directions;
- recognise and explore the uses of ICT in the home.
- use My World CD-ROM 'Dressing teddy and the Three Bears';

Design and making skills

- design and make equipment for the Bears' house, e.g. beds for bears, wallpaper, clocks and TV using a variety of materials;
- develop skills in construction by making three houses of different sizes using a variety of materials;

Creative development

The Three Bears role play will help the children to:

Exploring media and materials

- make observational pictures of teddy bears the children bring into school;
- make models of the bears using a variety of modelling materials distinguishing their sizes;

137

- design and make resources for the Three Bears' house using a selection of materials;

Appreciation

- look at paintings and sculptures of bears and discuss them;

Imagination

- engage in sequenced role play: to pretend to make a cup of tea or make porridge;
- use resources, costumes and props imaginatively to support their role play;
- play cooperatively to act out the Three Bears story or an invented story based around their cottage by changing the characters, sequence or the final outcome of the story;

Music

- sing songs that relate to bears;
- use instruments to make sounds that can represent the characters and use them in their role play.

Physical development

The Three Bears role play will help the children to:

Movement

- explore their movement by pretending to be the characters in the story;

Sense of space

- explore the ideas of personal space and fitting themselves into a confined space: the beds, chairs or making dens under blankets;
- develop an awareness of the needs of others to have space and share the limited space fairly;
- use directional and positional language in relation to real situations;

Using equipment and tools

- use large and small equipment safely with increased control and coordination;
- gain increasing control over clothes and simple fastenings.

Observational focus

Observe the children playing and ask them a variety of questions. Set up simple problem-solving situations connected to activities that happen in the Bears' house, and encourage the children to show you the answers and solutions.

1. Cannot remember any significant information/detail ☐
2. Can remember a small amount of information/detail ☐
3. Can give a full account of how various activities in the house are carried out ☐
4. Can extend play and create new characters and scenarios ☐

Table 30   The Three Bears

Date	Role play	Stories: Goldilocks and the Three Bears	
	Com./lang./lit. development	Mathematical development	Other areas of development
1	Listen to version 1 of the story and begin to sequence it. Discuss with the children what we need to retell the story. Develop the story and encourage the children to take over the different roles. Let the children share lots of different versions of the story.	Count the items we need to change the house area. Think about the size of all the objects and begin to use the correct mathematical language. Count, match and sort objects ready for Daddy, Mummy and Baby Bear. Use real items of food to share out between the bears.	Decorate the house area. Find or make three beds of suitable sizes. Make woodland scenes around it and through the windows and door. Ensure there are lots of simple masks in three sizes and clothes for the children to choose.
2	Compare the bears' day with the children's own. Are there any differences or similarities? What happens to them in the morning and at night-time. Let the children bring in their pyjamas and act out going to bed like the bear family. Describe their bed clothes. What did the bears need to do at night?	Say the days of the week. Look at different times of the day. Think about what happens at different times. Compare the lengths of the bears' beds and find a way to measure them using non-standard means of measurement.	Make Three Bears collage pictures with matching-sized objects. Stress the importance of sleeping and resting. Sing 'Goldilocks' Tale' thinking about comparative language.
3	When the bears wake up they wash themselves, keeping their bodies, teeth, hair and clothes clean. Read another version of the story.	Share out pretend biscuits and other items fairly. Increase the number of bears in the family and therefore the number of items. Make sets of items using one criterion then move on to more: big, green spoon.	Look at real bears and how they are often different from one another. How do they survive (hibernation) in the wild and what do they eat?
4	Think about and discuss the different	Measure out oats and water to make porridge	Consider safety in the kitchen when dealing

Table 30   *(Contd)*

Date	Role play	Stories: Goldilocks and the Three Bears	
	Com./lang./lit. development	Mathematical development	Other areas of development
	ways we make porridge. Follow instructions and make some, comparing the different sorts (write their opinions on paper bowls). Look at the writing on the cookbooks and packets. Pretend to make porridge in the bears' cottage. Read another version of the story.	using non-standard measures. Record the recipes and put them up in the bears' cottage. Photograph the sequence order for the recipe.	with hot items.
5	Discuss the bears' walk and what they may have seen. Extend the story in role adding new characters and situations with the adults recording the changes.	Plan a walk outdoors and predict what you may see. Draw a little plan of where you are going. Think about directions and distances to cover. Children take on roles and go outdoors to follow their planned route.	Look in books to find out what they may have seen in the woods. Make picture maps to illustrate the bears' outing.
6	The bears have a picnic. What will they need? Mummy Bear makes a shopping list and pretends to go to the shops to buy things. She pretends to organise sending invitations to the children's own bears and cook the food.	Count the number of bears invited and match to the food they make. Check the number of plates, straws and drinks.	Cook real food for a picnic. Think about what real bears would eat. Sing lots of other bear songs: 'The Teddy Bears' Picnic'.
7	Make name labels for bears. Have bears' picnic, share out the food, sing, play games and dance with the bears giving the instructions.	Sort children's bears into sets depending on size, texture, colour and clothes. Match the bears to children by reading their labels.	Children and bears set out their picnic in the outside play area. Children are reminded that they must think about politeness, sharing and tidying up after the event. Take photographs and tapes of event.

Table 30 *(Contd)*

Date	Role play	Stories: Goldilocks and the Three Bears	
	Com./lang./lit. development	Mathematical development	Other areas of development
8	Sequence photographs of the picnic, developing the skill to speak in sentences. The children put photographs and other work into a large book so they can retell the day over and over again.	Match the photograph of the bear with the child. Describe how they can tell it's the right match.	Use CD-ROM My World: 'Goldilocks and the Three Bears' program and sequence the story, printing off different sections of the story.

Snow White

Play situation

Create a play situation in the house corner and outside where the story of Snow White can be recreated and extended. If there is an outside area, it could represent the woods and castle where the wicked queen lives with her magic mirror. There is a cottage that comprises all of the usual house items but in sevens: cups, plates, dishes, cutlery, chairs, beds etc. where the dwarves live. There are costumes, crowns and masks that the children can wear to help them get into role. (See Table 31.)

> ### Introductory prompts
>
> Has anyone heard the story before?
> What characters are important in the story?
> Has anyone ever been to a forest? What was it like?
> What would you feel like if you were lost?
> Do you think the queen was kind? Why?

Possible roles

Snow White, seven dwarves, queen, servant, prince

Resources

Provide furniture, cooking equipment, tea sets, dressing-up clothes, telephones, seven place mats, dolls of different kinds to represent the dwarves, magic mirror made of tin foil, apples, ribbons, hair slides, masks, costumes, hats, books, labels, diaries, directories, notices, board, message pads, shopping list booklets, notebooks, writing tools, pretend TV, tape recorder, radio, household items with numbers such as cookers, telephones, clocks, computers, videos, and magazines, catalogues etc. which all use numbers for a variety of functions: prices, times, distances and identification. Have a selection of seven items that can be matched, sorted and positioned, and large pictures (child drawn) of trees, castle, woodland, cottage etc.

See Recommended reading for books about Snow White.

Link activities

Wash hands using different soaps, brushes and creams. Sequence the order of how hands are washed and know why they need to wash them.

Talk about the importance of sleeping and going to bed on time.

Dress and undress using fastenings, turning clothes from being inside out, using dolls and themselves. Understand the sequence of dressing.

Understand that all things are not good to eat and the dangers of poisonous things.

Explain the importance of always telling an adult where they are going to and never speaking to strangers.

Get ready to celebrate a wedding.

Potential learning opportunities

Personal, social and emotional development

The Snow White role play will help children to:

Disposition and attitude

- explore new learning experiences in the familiar setting of the home corner;
- initiate play and build upon their own interests, experiences and ideas to solve problems, e.g. not allowing Snow White to come into contact with the evil queen;

Self-confidence and self-esteem

- improve their self-confidence and begin to develop their own personal character and personality;
- reflect and chat about their play to children and adults;

Making relationships/behaviour/self-control

- express feelings and be sensitive to the needs of others, e.g. the dwarves wanting to care for and keep Snow White safe;

- develop relationships with children showing respect, interest and care for others (families and friends);
- share space fairly, take turns, develop self-made rules of behaviour and develop an ability to work as a member of a group;
- respond to and use appropriate social conventions such as please and thank you;

Self-care

- be aware of the need for personal hygiene to stay healthy;
- begin to develop appropriate social skills for eating together: table manners, clearing away, washing up and tidying up;
- be confident to select resources for play and ask a supporting adult for help if required;
- keep safe at home and when out and about.

Communication, language and literacy

The Snow White role play will help children to:

Speaking, listening and communicating

- speak and use appropriate body language to get attention, defend their own interests and be understood by friends and adults;
- name everyday objects, developing their language skills using adjectives to describe them and put them into simple sentences;
- begin to use language as a means of communicating giving simple instructions, asking for help and expressing opinions;
- develop questioning techniques using 'who': the queen asking the mirror, 'Who is the fairest of them all?' and 'where': 'Where is Snow White hiding?';
- remember the refrain from the story and use it: 'Mirror, mirror on the wall, who is the fairest of them all?';
- listen carefully to what others say when giving instructions and respond appropriately;
- use their language skills to take on and recreate familiar roles and experiences;
- discuss wishes and spells and whether they always have to be evil;

Reading

- listen to different versions of a traditional story (*Snow White* including the video);
- use real objects, puppets and sequence cards to retell and develop a sense of story sequence and identify the important characters in the story;
- retell the story and record it on tape sharing it with other children later;
- read a selection of other fairy or traditional stories to the children and compare the characters;
- gain an awareness of environmental print and understand it carries meaning: names on place mats at the cottage, labels on goods;
- read back their own writing in character;

Writing

- write a class book or little indivual zig-zag books to retell the story;
- begin to know that words have meaning and develop the need to be able to read and write;
- write in diaries, forms and letters in character, e.g. Snow White to the queen wanting to know why she is being so nasty;
- make and write invitations for Snow White's wedding using the children's real names.

Mathematical development

The Snow White role play will help children to:

Matching and sorting

- sort real objects within the dwarves' house according to colour which can be different for each dwarf;
- put toys away in appropriately and clearly labelled boxes and shelves;
- match objects using one-to-one correspondence: one spoon to one plate;
- sort objects according to two criteria, e.g. small red cups;
- sort objects according to function, e.g. something red to drink out of;
- match one to one, e.g. child to apple, belt or ribbon;
- match, recognise and write numbers around the home, e.g. on cookers, videos, catalogues;

Size

- match objects to the dwarves and Snow White depending on their size and the language related to it, e.g. big, little, long, short, and introduce the tools used for measuring length;

Number

- count forwards and backwards from zero to seven and seven to zero;
- count real objects around the house developing an ability to estimate;
- begin to recognise and write numbers and be aware of their order 0, 1, 2, 3, 4, 5, 6, 7;
- begin to investigate simple practical calculations involving addition and taking away when dwarves arrive home late or some want extra food;

Shape/space and measure

- find different 2-D and 3-D shapes in the cottage and castle environment and know some of their properties;

Length/weight/capacity/volume

- begin to use the language of quantity and weight when making food for the dwarves and length when measuring and sorting the queen's ribbons;

144

Time

- discuss the times of the day when different household activities occur: getting up for work, meals, bedtime and showers;
- begin to use the names for the days of the week and times on the clock;
- begin to develop the idea of a sequence of events, e.g. cooking or dressing.

Knowledge and understanding of the world

The Snow White role play will help children to:

Living processes/living things/environment

- develop an awareness of some of the characteristics and needs of living things (people);
- create a backdrop to the cottage by painting real animals and plants from research in books;

Materials and their properties

- explore the differences between hot and cold and be aware of the dangers involved.
- cook and observe food materials change when heated and cooled. Make food for dwarves, wedding feast and magic potions;

Sense of time

- be aware of how things have changed over time by comparing communication in Snow White's time to now.
- show an awareness of different times of the day;

Sense of place/ICT

- develop a sense of place by creating a picture map of Snow White's journey through the woods and around the cottage, and the journeys of the queen and prince. Use Roamer to develop an awareness of direction;
- begin to recognise and explore the uses of ICT in the home;

Design and making skills

- develop skills in construction by making the two houses (castle and cottage) of different sizes using a variety of materials;
- design and make equipment for the dwarves' cottage and the castle, e.g. seven beds for dwarves, seven place mats, wallpaper, clocks, using a variety of materials.

Creative development

The Snow White role play will help children to:

Exploring media and materials

- make pictures and models of the characters using lots of different media and modelling materials concentrating on facial features, making some happy and kind while others are evil-looking;
- design and make resources for the role-play area using a wide selection of materials, e.g. the castle grey and grim, and the cottage bright and surrounded by natural living things;

Appreciation

- look at paintings from the film and books and discuss how the characters change in appearance;

Imagination

- use their imagination and develop representation in their play, e.g. using familiar items to represent the queen's poisonous objects;
- engage in sequenced role play, e.g. pretend to make a cup of tea or a magic potion.
- use resources, costumes and props imaginatively to support their role play;
- play cooperatively to act out the story or an invented story based around the props;
- extend the story by changing the characters, sequence or the final outcome of the story;

Music

- sing songs from the video;
- use instruments to make sounds that can represent the characters and use them in play.

Physical development

The Snow White role play will help children to:

Movement

- explore their movement by pretending to be the characters in the story and change their speed and the direction they travel in;

Sense of space

- develop an awareness of the needs of others to have space;

- explore the idea of hiding from something or someone that frightens them in a small confined space using boxes and blankets;
- begin to use directional and positional language in relation to real objects and people in the role-play scenario;

Using equipment and tools

- begin to use large and small equipment safely with increased control and coordination while making props for the area;
- gain increasing control over clothes and simple fastenings while dressing up.

Observational focus

Observe the children at play and ask them a variety of questions. Set up simple problem-solving situations connected to activities that happen in the story, and assess how they answer them.

1. Cannot remember any significant information/detail ☐
2. Can remember a small amount of information/detail ☐
3. Can give a full account of how various activities in the house are carried out ☐
4. Can extend the play by creating new characters and scenarios ☐

Table 31 Snow White

Date	Role play	Stories: Snow White and the Seven Dwarves	
	Com./lang./lit. development	Mathematical development	Other areas of development
1	Read version 1 of the story. Discuss the characters and roles to play and begin to identify the main events. Begin to sequence them. Think about what props they need. The two areas, the castle (grey and dark) and the cottage (bright and surrounded by plants and animals).	Children find seven of everything for the house (plates, cups, knives, forks, spoons, dishes, place mats, chairs, beds, hats). Set up the area so all these things are visible. Count and match items to each dwarf. Put items into sets e.g. seven cups, seven hats.	Make a magic mirror using tin foil. Think about its size and shape. Decorate areas with paintings and pictures of plants, trees and wild animals. Discuss the idea of good and bad actions.
2	Children learn the queen's question to the mirror: 'Mirror, mirror on the wall, who is the	Make up a tray of ribbons of lots of different colours, lengths and materials for the	Make a picture map to show Snow White's journey. Why is it important not to talk to

147

Table 31   *(Contd)*

Date	Role play	Stories: Snow white and the seven dwarves	
	Com./lang./lit. development	Mathematical development	Other areas of development
	fairest of them all?' and the mirror answers... Begin to act out the story with some adult support.	children to sort and match.	strangers?
3	Read another version of the story and compare. Are the pictures of the characters the same? Do the same events happen?	Make a collection of hair decorations for the children to sort and match.	The dwarves love and care for Snow White and want to look after her. How?
4	Think about magic spells and what other spells the queen could have made. Do they always need to be evil and nasty? Watch selected parts of the video. Compare to stories. Make and write invitations to Snow White's wedding.	Count and sort a large bag of apples. Find one with the correct colouring.	Investigate the idea of being happy and sad. Discuss that sometimes pets and people die and any experiences the children have had. Discuss weddings and how we celebrate them. Hold a pretend wedding with bride, groom and guests.
5	Try to create a different end to the story, perhaps having Snow White as a boy wanting to be not the fairest but the strongest. Think if you need any new props. Record their story for children to share later.	Count forwards and backwards from 7. Make 0–7 number lines on computer. Put large cut-out 7s all over the cottage.	Use outside play area as well to create your new story. Paint pictures of the new story.

The Three Tittle Pigs

Play situation

Create a play situation with three houses made of different materials where the story can be recreated and extended. Each house comprises all of the usual house items but in ones this time: cup, plate, dish, cutlery, chair, bed and a cooking pot etc. The three houses could be drawn on a rotating white board, either by the children or with the help of an adult. There are costumes and masks that the children can wear to help them get into role. If there is an outside area available it can be used to complement the play. (See Table 32.)

Introductory prompts

Were the pigs happy at home?
What is your house made of?
Do you think the pigs were sad to leave?
How do you think the pigs felt?
What do you think they needed to take with them?

Possible roles

Mummy Pig, three little pigs, tradesmen, wolf.

Resources

Supply the three houses with furniture, cooking equipment, tea sets, dressing-up clothes, vacuum cleaner, cleaning equipment, place mats, irons, masks, costumes, books, labels, diaries, directories, notices, board, message pads, shopping list booklets, notebooks, writing tools, intercom telephones, pretend TV, tape recorder, radio, pig toys and puppets, household items with numbers: cookers, telephones, clocks, computers, videos, magazines, catalogues etc. which all use numbers for a variety of functions (price, time, distance, identification).

Have a large picture (child drawn) of countryside and the houses made of straw, wood and bricks.

See Recommended reading for books about pigs and wolves.

Link activities

Make houses using different materials.
Dressing and undressing: learn the order of dressing using fastenings and turning clothes from being inside out. Use dolls and toys as well as themselves.
Hold Polly Pig's birthday party (celebrating).
Talk about wolves and how they live.
Discuss pigs and farming.

Potential learning opportunities

Personal, social and emotional development

The Three Pigs role play will help children to:

Disposition and attitude

- explore new learning experiences in the familiar settings of three different houses;
- initiate play and build upon their own personal interests and experiences;
- begin to reflect on their own play to children and adults;

Self-confidence and self-esteem

- improve their self-confidence and begin to develop their own character and personality;
- enjoy themselves and play confidently together as a group;
- develop their own identity and that of their characters;
- identify which events make them sad and happy;

Making relationships/behaviour/self-control

- express their feelings and be sensitive to the needs of others (the third little pig wants to care for his brothers and keep them safe), showing interest, respect and care;
- share space fairly, take turns, develop self-made rules of behaviour and develop an ability to work as a member of a group;

Self-care

- be aware of personal hygiene and develop appropriate social skills for eating together: table manners, and clearing away, washing up and tidying up;
- keep safe at home and out and about, always letting an adult know where they are.

Communication, language and literacy

The Three Pigs role play will help children to:

Speaking, listening and communicating

- speak clearly and use appropriate body language to get attention, to defend their own interests and to be understood by friends and adults;
- name everyday objects and develop their language skills using adjectives to describe them and put them into simple sentences;
- use language as a means of communicating, giving simple instructions, asking for help and expressing opinions;

- develop questioning techniques using how, when, where and why;
- listen carefully to what others say when giving instructions and respond appropriately;
- remember the refrain from the story: 'Little pig, little pig, let me come in' and use it appropriately in play;
- use their language skills to take on and recreate familiar roles and experiences from the story;
- use intercom telephones so that the pigs can warn each other of the wolf's whereabouts;

Reading

- listen to different versions of a traditional story: *The Three Little Pigs*;
- develop a sense of story sequence and the characters that make the story;
- use real objects, puppets and sequence cards to retell the story and develop a sense of story structure and begin to identify the main characters;
- encourage them to retell the story and record it on tape. Listen to each other retelling the story;
- share their own writing with peers and adults and try reading it back in character;
- think about the 'p' sound and party activities: parcels, paper, poppers, pass the parcel, party games and party food;

Writing

- write a class book to retell the story from the pigs' point of view, the wolf's and Mummy Pig's;
- begin to know that words have meaning and develop the need to be able to read and write;

151

- make and write letters and party invitations in character from one pig to another.

Mathematical development

The Three Pigs role play will help children to:

Matching and sorting

- match and sort real objects within each pig's house considering one-to-one correspondence: blue spoon to blue plate, a different colour for each pig, and an object's function: something red to drink out of;
- put toys away in appropriately labelled places;
- match, recognise and write numbers around the home, e.g. on cookers, videos, catalogues;
- match party items to each pig: crackers, balloons and party poppers;

Number

- count forwards and backwards, beginning to be able to recognise some numerals;
- count objects around the house, developing an ability to estimate: count the number of pigs at the party and the candles on the birthday cake;
- begin to investigate simple practical calculations in the pig's houses involving addition and taking away;

Shape/space and measure

- find different 2-D and 3-D shapes in the pigs' houses and the environment and know some of their properties;

Length/weight/capacity/volume

- begin to use the language of quantity and weight when making food for the party;

Time

- discuss times of the day when different household activities occur: meals, bedtime and showers;
- develop the idea of getting up and going to work;
- use the names for the days of the week and times on the clock: look in the book *What's the Time Mr Wolf?*;
- begin to sequence events considering time.

Knowledge and understanding of the world

The Three Pigs role play will help children to:

Living processes/living thing/environment

- develop an awareness of some of the characteristics and needs of living things, e.g. pigs and wolves;
- create a backdrop to the houses by painting plants, trees and flowers in the fields using non-fiction reading material and photographs;

Materials and their properties

- discriminate between the different building materials, e.g. straw, sticks and brick, sand and other materials, and investigate building with them;

Physical processes

- investigate the differences between hot and cold and be aware of the dangers involved when they cook food for the party. Observe how materials change when heated or cooled;
- look at household appliances that use electricity and understand the dangers;

Sense of time

- be aware of how things have changed over time and investigate old kitchen equipment found in the pigs' homes;
- be aware of the different times of the day;

Sense of place/ICT

- develop a sense of place by creating a picture map of the pigs' story and use Roamer to reinforce directions;
- use a tape recorder to record their sequenced stories;
- recognise and explore the uses of ICT in the home;
- use 'The Three Little Pigs' CD-ROM to support the story;

Design and making skills

- design and make three houses for the pigs, taking into account the suitability of the materials chosen;
- design and make equipment for the three houses: chairs, tables, beds, wallpaper, clocks and TV, using a variety of materials, and appreciate that designs and models can be modified to make them more appropriate for the task in question.

Creative development

The Three Pigs role play will help children to:

Exploring media and materials

- make pictures and models of the characters using lots of different media and modelling materials distinguishing their sizes;

- design and make resources for the role-play area using a selection of materials;

Appreciation

- look at paintings and photographs of homes and the animals in the story and discuss them;

Imagination

- use their imagination and available resources to develop representation in their play;
- choose costumes and masks to complement their story: each child has a pig and wolf mask in their tray to use in role-play area;
- engage in sequenced role play, e.g. pretending to make a birthday cake;
- play cooperatively to act out the story or an invented story based around the props;
- extend the story by changing the characters, sequence or the final outcome of the story;

Music

- Sing songs: 'Who's afraid of the Big Bad Wolf', 'Huff Puff';
- use instruments to make sounds that can represent the characters and use them in play.

Physical development

The Three Pigs role play will help children to:

Movement

- explore their movement by pretending to be the characters in the story;

Sense of space

- develop an awareness of the needs of others to have space;
- hide from something that frightens them and make themselves very small;
- begin to use directional and positional language in relation to real situations;

Using equipment and tools

- use a range of large construction material safely (large boxes and kits);
- begin to use large and small equipment safely with increased control and coordination and gain increasing control over clothes and simple fastenings.

Observational focus

Observe and ask the children a variety of questions. Give them simple problem-solving situations connected to activities that happen in the story. Assess how they play and answer some simple questions.

1. Cannot remember any significant information/detail ☐
2. Can remember a small amount of information /detail. ☐
3. Can give a full account of how various activities in the house are carried out. ☐
4. Can extend the play by creating new characters and scenarios. ☐

Table 32 The Three Little Pigs

Date	Role play	Story: The Three Little Pigs	
	Com./lang./lit. development	Mathematical development	Other areas of development
1	Read version 1 of the story. Discuss the characters and roles to play and begin to identify the main events. Begin to sequence them. Think about what props we need and the three areas, one for each pig.	Look carefully at the different shapes of the houses in the story. Try making them in miniature. Draw shapes of houses on a rolling white board for instant props. Think about the size of the wolf compared to the pigs and the houses.	Plan and construct houses for pigs using appropriate materials. Start with the straw. Fit out with household items. Decorate areas around with paintings and pictures of plants, trees and wild animals.

Table 32   *(Contd)*

Date	Role play	Story: The Three Little Pigs	
	Com./lang./lit. development	Mathematical development	Other areas of development
2	Children learn the wolf's question to the pigs and their reply. They begin to act out the story with some adult support. Have intercom telephones so that the pigs can communicate with each other.	Discuss the shapes children find in the houses. Group three of everything for each house: plates, cups, knives and forks, spoons, dishes, place mats, chairs, beds and hats. Set up the area so all these things are visible. Count and match items one to each pig using matching colours.	Design and make the house of sticks. Decorate and fit with household items. Make masks (pigs and wolves) so that the children can play freely in the area.
3	Read another version of the story and compare. Are the pictures of the characters the same? Do the same events happen? Use puppets to tell the story. Sing 'Huff Puff' song.	Look at the shape of the bricks. Build structures with construction kits to test the different shapes. Use ordinal numbers when referring to the pigs: first, second and third.	Design and construct the house of bricks. Test them to see which material is the strongest and which house is able to stay up the longest.
4	Write invitations to Polly Pig's party ('p'sound). Give the guests names that have 'p' as an initial sound.	Count the pig guests, parcels, poppers and food. Count the candles on the cake. Identify the numbers on the birthday cards.	Develop the party idea with games and 'p' activities: pass the parcel, pop, paper, party poppers and more party games.
5	Try to create a different end to the story, perhaps with the wolf managing to get into one of the houses or someone coming to help them. Think if you need any new props. Record their story for children to share later.	Count forwards and backwards from three. Make 0–3 number lines on computer. Put large cut-out numbers over the houses: 0, 1, 2, 3.	Use outside play area as well to create your new story. Paint pictures of the new story.

The Three Billy Goats Gruff

Play situation

Create a play situation in the role-play area where the story of the Three Billy Goats Gruff can be recreated and extended. There may be outside or inside areas to represent the fields, river and bridge. The bridge can be made of different materials depending on what the children choose. There are costumes and masks that the children can wear to help them get into role. (See Table 33.)

Introductory prompts

Has anyone ever been over a bridge? Take the children to a bridge if possible.
What was it like?
Why do we have them?
Do you know any stories/songs that have a bridge in?
Why do you need to be careful on a bridge?

Possible roles

Big Billy Goat, Middle-sized Billy Goat, Little Billy Goat, troll and people from the village

Resources

Provide the role-play area with construction kits, benches, see-saws, large pictures (child drawn) of trees, river and fields, masks and costumes, notebooks, writing tools, TV, tape recorder, radio, telephones, clocks, computers, videos, magazines, catalogues etc. which use numbers for a variety of functions (price, time, distance, identification).

See Recommended reading for books about the Three Billy Goats Gruff.

Link activities

Looking at bridges in books and use ICT.
Think about caring for farm animals and look at their characteristics.
Discuss good and bad behaviour.
Make collages of the three goats and troll giving each an identity.

Potential learning opportunities

Personal, social and emotional development

The Three Billy Goats Gruff role play will help the children to:

Disposition and attitude

- explore new learning experiences in what may be the unfamiliar setting of the countryside;
- enjoy themselves with their friends and supporting adults and begin to reflect on their play;

Self-confidence and self-esteem

- improve their self-confidence and begin to develop their own personal character and personality;
- initiate play and build upon their own interests, experiences and ideas to solve problems relating to the story;

Making relationships/behaviour/self-control

- use imaginative play to express their feelings, be sensitive to the needs of others and develop relationships where they show respect, interest and care;
- use the Three Billy Goats Gruff to explore the concept of good and bad behaviour;
- share space fairly, take turns, develop self-made rules of behaviour and develop an ability to work as a member of a group;

Self-care

- be aware of safety issues, always telling an adult where they are going and not talking to or accepting gifts from strangers;
- dress and undress when changing roles and costumes.

Communication, language and literacy

The Three Billy Goats Gruff role play will help the children to:

Speaking, listening and communicating

- speak clearly and use appropriate body language to get attention, to defend their own interests and be understood by friends and supporting adults;
- develop questioning skills, give simple instructions, ask for help and express opinions (telephone the troll and ask him to let the village use the bridge);
- listen carefully to what others say when giving instructions and respond appropriately;
- use their language skills to take on and recreate familiar roles and experiences.

Try filming the story (video cameras) or interviewing the troll to find out how he feels;

- respond to and use appropriate social conventions such as please and thank you;

Reading

- listen to different versions of a traditional story (*The Three Billy Goats Gruff*), retell the story and tape it;
- listen to each other retelling the story and develop a sense of story sequence and identify the main characters that make the story;
- use real objects, puppets and sequence cards to retell it;
- gain an awareness of environmental print and understand it carries meaning: make warning signs about the troll;
- read back their own writing in character;

Writing

- know that words have meaning and develop the need to be able to read and write;
- write individual little zig-zag books to retell the story;
- write letters to the council about the troll or write to the troll personally;
- write instructions on how to make different bridges with illustrations and photographs;
- make and write invitations for the village to cross over the bridge for a celebration and party;

Mathematical development

The Three Billy Goats Gruff role play will help the children to:

Matching and sorting

- sort objects according to two or three criteria, e.g. small, middle-sized or large Billy Goats Gruff/small, middle-sized or large cups/red, yellow or blue colour etc.;

Size

- match objects to goats depending on their size;
- order three objects: make sets of three big objects and three small objects;
- think about the size of the goats and the language related to them, e.g. big, little, long, short, and use some simple tools to measure length;

Number

- count objects around the house developing an ability to estimate up to three and beyond;

- begin to recognise numbers up to three and beyond;
- begin to investigate simple practical calculations involving addition and taking away;
- understand ordinal numbers while waiting in queues: first, second and third;

Shape/space and measure

- find different 2-D and 3-D shapes on the bridge and use this knowledge to help them design and build bridges;

Length/weight/capacity/volume

- use the language of length to measure and construct bridges;

Time

- discuss times of the day, begin to name the days of the week and the times on the clock;
- begin to develop the idea of a sequence of events;

Knowledge and understanding of the world

The Three Billy Goats Gruff role play will help the children to:

Living processes/living things/environment

- know some of the characteristics and needs of living things (goats and other farm animals);

Materials and their properties

- discriminate between different materials: plastic, wood, metal, glass, while making bridges;
- distinguish between man-made and natural materials while making bridges;
- appreciate that materials have different properties that can be used for different functions, explore the properties of different building materials and kits for making bridges;

Physical processes

- gain some awareness of the forces that can act upon a bridge;
- investigate whether the troll floats or sinks;

ICT

- use cameras and tapes to record the story and interviews with the characters;

Construction

- design and build model bridges with a variety of materials and construction kits and adapt them to solve any problems;

Design

- choose appropriate materials, tools and equipment to make the bridges;
- develop and make a model for a purpose (child to be able to walk across) considering artefacts, systems and environment;

Sense of time

- look at photographs and paintings of old bridges and begin to develop an understanding of how they are different from modern ones;
- show an awareness of the times of the day;

Sense of place

- look at photographs of bridges that are local and worldwide and record what they find;
- understand that a bridge is a means of crossing an obstacle: water, railway or road;
- draw a picture map to show where the bridge was and the route the goats took from the village;

Creative development

The Three Billy Goats Gruff role play will help the children to:

Exploring media and materials

- make observational pictures and models of bridges and goats;
- design and make resources for the role-play area using a selection of materials (paint or make models of the troll);

Appreciation

- look at paintings and photographs of bridges and discuss them;

Imagination

- use resources and props imaginatively to support their role play;
- play cooperatively choosing costumes to complement and act out the Three Billy Goats Gruff story with a group of friends;
- extend the story by changing the characters, sequence or the final outcome of the story;

Music

- sing songs that relate to the topics: *Silver Burdett Book 1*, 'London Bridge is falling down', 'Three singing pigs', 'The three billy goats gruff';
- use instruments to make sounds that can represent the characters and use them in play;

Physical development

The Three Billy Goats Gruff role play will help the children to:

Movement

- explore their movement by pretending to be different characters in the story;
- develop skills of balancing along narrow bridges;

Sense of space

- develop an awareness of the needs of others to have space;
- make new dens for the goats on the other side of the bridge out of boxes and blankets;
- begin to use directional and positional language in relation to real situations;

Using equipment and tools

- use large and small equipment safely with increased control and coordination while they construct the bridges;
- gain increasing control over clothes and simple fastenings.

Observational focus

Observe the children playing and ask them a variety of questions. Give them simple problem-solving situations connected to activities that happen on the bridge, and encourage them to show you them and try to solve the problems.

1. Cannot remember any significant information/detail ☐
2. Can remember a small amount of information/detail ☐
3. Can give a full account of how various activities in the house are carried out ☐
4. Can extend play by creating new characters and scenarios ☐

Table 33 Three Billy Goats Gruff

Date	Role play	Story: Three Billy Goats Gruff	
	Com./lang./lit. development	Mathematical development	Other areas of development
1	Read version 1 of the story. Discuss the characters and roles to play and begin to identify the main events. Begin to sequence them. Think about what props they will need for the two areas: the bridge with the stream running underneath and the field (bright and green).	Children make goat masks: one small, one middle-sized and one big. Order children according to size. Order other objects connected to the role play by size: goat's bells. Think about the sizes of the bridges and begin to use the correct mathematical language.	We need bridges to cross obstacles. Look in books, video and ICT to find out about them. Design a bridge. Use a variety of construction kits and real materials to test ideas. Decorate areas with paintings and pictures of fields, trees and wild animals.
2	Children learn the troll's question 'Who is that trip, trap, trapping on my bridge?' and the goats' replies. Begin to act out the story with some adult support.	Investigate floating and sinking in the water tray using a selection of objects. Record on a chart and count how many sink and how many float.	Use a variety of materials to make a troll. Design a simple costume/mask for the troll. How did he feel? How did he make the goats feel? Discuss the idea of good and bad characters. Make models of him out of a variety of materials and predict whether he will float or sink.
3	Read another version of the story and compare. Are the pictures of the characters the same? Do the same events happen? Look in non-fiction books and find out about mountain goats and how they live in the mountains.	Count the footsteps across the bridge. Have different numbers of goats going over the bridge. Count the number of horns, noses, legs etc.	Practise balancing across the bridge. Try bridges of different widths and lengths. Discuss whether you think the goats are frightened. Have you ever been frightened? Do you think they are brave?
4	Use instruments to represent the characters or use different voices (loud or soft). Play independently in area.	Think about ordinal numbers. Make queues and use the correct language: first to fifth.	Look at photographs and paintings of bridges both modern and old. Paint and take photographs of some of the bridges the children have made.

Table 33   *(Contd)*

Date	Role play	Story: Three Billy Goats Gruff	
	Com./lang./lit. development	Mathematical development	Other areas of development
5	Create a different end to the story. Perhaps the troll caught one of the goats, another character came to help or the troll was kind. Think if you need any new props. Record their story for children to share later.	The goats have a party and invite all of the village. Count and match party items so they have one each (balloons, plates, cups, food etc).	Use outside play area as well to create your new story. Paint pictures of the new story. Sing 'London Bridge is falling down'.

Red Riding Hood

Play situation

Create a play situation with two houses in two different locations, perhaps one outside and one inside, the latter to be Grandma's house. Each house comprises all of the usual house items: cups, plates, dishes, cutlery, chairs and beds. One of the houses could be drawn on a revolving white board, either by the children or with the help of an adult. There are costumes and masks that the children can wear to help them get into role. (See Table 34.)

Introductory prompts

Why did Red Riding Hood go through the woods by herself?
Why did her mummy not go with her?
How did she carry everything? Can you think of a better carrier?
Do you think it was safe to walk through the woods? Why?
Have you ever been in woodland?
What was it like?
Would you have spoken to the wolf?
Do you think she should have carried on going on her journey after meeting the wolf? Why?

Possible roles

Mummy, Red Riding Hood, grandmother, woodcutter, wolf

164

Resources

Provide the two houses with furniture, cooking equipment, tea sets, dressing-up clothes, telephones, hairdryers, vaccum cleaners, cleaning equipment, place mats, large pictures (child drawn) of woodland. Include a basket, masks, costumes, books, magazines, labels, diaries, directories, notices, board, message pads, shopping list booklets, notebooks, writing tools, intercom telephones, pretend TV, tape recorder and radio, household items with numbers such as cookers, telephones, clocks, computers, videos, and magazines, catalogues etc. which all use numbers for a variety of functions (price, time, distance, identification). Have a selection of items that can be matched and sorted depending on a variety of criteria: colour, size, type and pattern.

A group of objects can be used to explore the concepts of position: cups, saucers, spoons, knives, forks etc., soft toys, dolls, large toys.

See Recommended reading for books about Red Riding Hood.

Link activities

Make collages of the two houses using different materials.
Dress and undress and learn the order of dressing using fastening, turning clothes from being inside out. Use dolls and toys as well as themselves for characters.
Look at the different types of trees around school.
Look at woodland pictures focusing on flowers.
Discuss environmental care and pollution in the local area and worldwide.

Potential learning opportunities

Personal, social and emotional development

The Red Riding Hood role play will help the children to:

Disposition and attitude

- explore their new learning environment of a woodland and the more familiar setting of the home corner;

Self-confidence and self-esteem

- improve their confidence and begin to develop their own personal character and personality;
- initiate play and build upon their own interests, experiences (lost in a supermarket) and ideas to solve problems (finding her way through the woods);
- reflect and chat about their play to children and adults;

Making relationships/behaviour/self-control

- express how they feel and be sensitive to the needs and feelings of others by modifying their own behaviour if appropriate, exploring Mummy's, wolf's, Red Riding Hood's and the woodcutter's feelings during play;
- develop relationships with other children to show, respect, interest and care for others;
- use limited space fairly, take turns, develop this into self-made rules of behaviour and an ability to work as a member of a group;

Self-care

- reinforce personal hygiene by washing hands before they eat;
- begin to develop appropriate social skills for eating together: table manners, and clearing away, washing up and tidying up;
- keep safe at home and out and about by not talking to or accepting gifts from strangers, and not going out without telling an adult where they are going and with whom.

Communication, language and literacy

The Red Riding Hood role play will help the children to:

Speaking, listening and communicating

- speak clearly and use appropriate body language to get attention, to defend their own interests and be understood by friends and adults;
- name everyday objects found in the house: plate, table, and in the countryside and develop their language skills to put them into simple sentences;
- begin to use language as a means of communicating giving simple directions, asking for help and expressing opinions;
- listen carefully to what others say when giving instructions and respond appropriately (directions to Grandma's house);
- develop an understanding of questions using how, when, where and why. Remember the refrain from the story and use it: 'Oh Grandma! What big . . .' and encourage the children to make up their own;
- use their language skills to take on and recreate familiar roles and experiences (mum, little girl etc.);
- discuss the route she takes and how she could have been more careful;
- how would a mobile phone have helped? Tape conversations the characters may have had;
- respond to and use appropriate social conventions such as please and thank you.

Reading

- listen to different versions of a traditional story (*Little Red Riding Hood*).
- encourage the children to retell the story (tape them) and listen to each other retelling the story. Develop a sense of story sequence and the characters that make the story by the use of real objects, puppets and sequence cards;

- gain an awareness of environmental print and understand it carries meaning (looking at maps and plans);
- read the children's own writing and pictures in character;
- look at capital letters and how they are used for all names and places;
- think about 'r' sound and how it occurs in the story. Make sentences using 'r' words.

Writing

- write a group zig-zag book to retell the story from different points of view (Grandma, wolf, Red Riding Hood);
- begin to know that words have meaning (danger, stop etc.) and develop the need to be able to read and write;
- write a letter and draw pictures on Grandma's behalf saying thank you to the people who helped her and inviting them to tea at her house;

Mathematical development

The Red Riding Hood role play will help the children to:

Matching and sorting

- sort real objects in Grandma's house and in the basket according to various criteria;
- put toys away in appropriate clearly labelled places (tea set, beds etc.);
- match, recognise and write numbers around the home: on cookers, videos and catalogues;
- ensure there are enough tea items for the guests (Mummy, Red Riding Hood, Dad, woodcutter);

Number

- count forwards and backwards beginning to recognise some numbers;
- count objects around the house developing an ability to estimate: number of sweets in a bag, cakes on a plate or flowers in a bunch;
- begin to investigate simple practical calculations involving addition and taking away: the total number of items in a basket, one more or less than;

Shape/space and measure

- find different 2-D and 3-D shapes in the houses and the environment and begin to identify some of their properties;

Length, weight, capacity and volume

- begin to use the language of quantity when making food for the party;
- begin to measure the distance covered using a unit of non-standard measure, e.g. footsteps;

Time

- discuss times of the day when different household activities occur: meals, bedtime and showers, and develop the idea of getting up and going to work, doing jobs around the home;
- begin to use the names for the days of the week and times on the clock ('What's the time, Mr Wolf?').

Knowledge and understanding of the world

The Red Riding Hood role play will help the children to:

Living processes/living things/environment

- develop an awareness of some of the characteristics and needs of living things (differences and similarities between wolves and people, different species of flowers);
- create a backdrop to Grandma's cottage by painting plants and fields (use children's non-fiction books about flora to help them;

Materials and their properties

- discriminate between different building materials when making props for the houses out of card, boxes and scraps of wood, e.g. Grandma's bed;

Physical processes

- explore the differences between hot and cold and be aware of the dangers involved when they cook, and observe materials changing when heated or cooled (cooking food for tea at Grandma's);
- discuss the functions of some household appliances that use electricity and be aware of their dangers;

Sense of time

- compare Grandma's house with Red Riding Hood's looking at old kitchen equipment in the cottage and modern equipment in Red Riding Hood's house. Be aware of how things have changed;

Sense of place/ICT

- develop a sense of place by creating a picture map of Red Riding Hood's journey. Use Roamer to develop an awareness of directions;
- recognise and explore the uses of ICT in the home;
- encourage the children to take photographs of the characters and the backdrop using a digital camera;

Design and making skills

- design and make the two houses for the characters taking into account the suitability of the materials they have chosen;
- design rooms and begin to make and gather equipment for the two houses: chairs, tables, beds, wallpaper, clocks and TV using a variety of materials and begin to appreciate that designs and models can be modified to make them more appropriate for the task in question.

Creative development

The Red Riding Hood role play will help the children to:

Exploring media and materials

- make life-size pictures and models of the characters using lots of different media and modelling materials distinguishing their sizes;
- design the background using photographs and other non-fiction materials;

Appreciation

- look at paintings and photographs of woodland and countryside;

Imagination

- use their imagination and develop representation in their play;
- engage in sequenced role play, e.g. to pretend to make tea;
- play cooperatively to act out the story or an invented story based around the props and use them imaginatively to support their play;
- use costumes and masks to complement their story (each child has a wolf mask in their tray to use in role-play area);
- extend the story by changing the characters, sequence or the final outcome of the story;

Music

- sing songs: 'Who's afraid of the big bad wolf?'.
- use instruments to make sounds that can represent the characters and use them in play.

Physical development

The Red Riding Hood role play will help the children to:

Movement

- explore their movement by pretending to be the characters in the story (wolf running on four legs, Red Riding Hood skipping, Grandma moving slowly);

169

- change the speed of movement depending on how the character feels (the more frightened, the faster they go);

Sense of space

- develop an awareness of the need for others to have space;
- develop the idea of hiding from something that they pretend frightens them, e.g. hide and seek;
- begin to use directional and positional language in relation to real situations within the role play;

Using equipment and tools

- use a range of large construction material safely (large boxes etc.);
- begin to use large and small equipment safely with increased control and coordination (scissors, brushes, pencils, knives and forks etc.);
- gain increasing control over clothes and simple fastenings (zips, buttons, press studs, velcro, laces and ties).

Observational focus

Ask the children a variety of questions, and set up simple problem-solving situations connected to activities that happen in the story, and assess how they show you or answer them.

1. Cannot remember any significant information/detail ☐
2. Can remember a small amount of information/detail ☐
3. Can give a full account of how various activities in the house are carried out ☐
4. Can develop the play by creating new characters and scenarios ☐

Table 34   Red Riding Hood

Date	Role play	Story: Red Riding Hood	
	Com./lang./lit. development	Mathematical development	Other areas of development
1	Read version 1 of the story. Discuss the characters and roles to play and begin to identify the main events and to sequence it. Think about what props we need. The two areas, the home and Grandma's cottage (bright and surrounded by plants and animals)	Make a list of items that Grandma needs. Children count the items Mum puts into the basket (use real objects). See if the children can remember what is under the cover.	Set up areas. (Use white board for instant props.) Children make masks of the wolf and the other characters so they can experience playing all the roles.

Table 34   *(Contd)*

Date	Role play	Story: Red Riding Hood	
	Com./lang./lit. development	Mathematical development	Other areas of development
	and a woodland area in between.		
2	Discuss how the wolf knew where to go. How did he manage to get to Grandma's first? Think about capital letters in Red Riding Hood's name. What sound do they make? Can you think of any other 'r' words in the story (red, ride, run, rabbit, rose, rain) to make sentences for role play?	Think about directions and how to describe a simple route using mathematical language. Count the flowers that she picks. Think about their colour and shape. Try to classify them.	Paint pictures of wild flowers using books, photographs and the Internet. Make a picture map to show Red Riding Hood's journey. Emphasise the importance of not talking to strangers.
3	What happens when the wolf gets to Grandma's cottage? Read another version of the story and compare. Are the pictures of the characters the same? Do the same events happen?	Let the children spot and count rabbits. Think of the shape of Grandma's spectacles and make a variety for her to wear.	Make collage rabbits and hide them in the background for the children to spot and count. Red Riding Hood is kind but what about the wolf? Read *Wolf: How Real Wolves Live* Think about good and evil in stories.
4	Think about the questions that Red Riding Hood asks the wolf. Learn the refrains: 'What big eyes you have Grandma.' Encourage the children to create their own refrains.	Set the table for tea ensuring you have enough cups and plates for Grandma's tea party.	Investigate the idea of being frightened and sometimes having to be brave. Why do some people wear spectacles?
5	Try to create a different end to the story. Perhaps have Red Riding Hood being nasty and mean and the wolf being kind. Think if you need any new props. Record their story for the class to share later.	Discuss the position of the new props using mathematical language.	Use outside play area as well to create your new story. Paint pictures of the new story. Emphasise the importance of looking after the environment.

Table 34   Blank table form

Date	Role play		
	Com./lang./lit. development	Mathematical development	Other areas of development
1			
2			
3			
4			
5			

Appendix: Tina Bruce's 12 features of play

In order to increase our knowledge of play, and develop practice wisdom, we need to become skilled and effective observers of play.

(Bruce 2001)

Tina Bruce identified 12 features of play which she suggests we use as a window on play to help to inform us how much real play is taking place.

1. In their play, children use their first-hand experiences that they have in life.
2. Children make up rules as they play, and so keep control of their play.
3. Children make play props.
4. Children choose to play. They cannot be made to play.
5. Children rehearse the future in their play.
6. Children pretend when they play.
7. Children play alone sometimes.
8. Children and/or adults play together in parallel, associatively, or cooperatively in pairs or groups.
9. Each player has a personal play agenda, although they may not be aware of this.
10. Children playing will be deeply involved, and difficult to distract from their deep learning. Children at play wallow in their learning.
11. Children try out their most recent learning, skills and competencies when they play. They seem to celebrate what they know.
12. Children at play co-ordinate their ideas, feelings, and make sense of relationships with their family, friends and culture. When play is coordinated it flows along in a sustained way. It is called 'free-flow' play.

(Developed from Bruce (1991 and 1996) and taken from Bruce, T. (2001) *Learning Through Play: Babies, Toddlers and the Foundation Years*. Hodder & Stoughton).

Tina Bruce suggests that if you see more than seven of these indicators in a play situation then you are observing quality play.

RECOMMENDED READING

House

Non-fiction

Cartwright, S. and Civardi, A. (2002) *Usborne First Experiences, Moving House.* London: Usborne.

Jackman, W. (1991) *My Book About Houses and Homes.* Hove: Wayland.

Tanner, G. and Wood, T. (1992) *Olden Homes Cooking.* London: A. & C. Black.

Tanner, G. and Wood, T. (1992) *Olden Homes Washing.* London: A. & C. Black.

Theme for Early Years Homes. London: Scholastic.

Thompson, R. (1994) *Changing Times Homes.* London: Watts.

Fiction

Adamson, J. and G. *Topsy and Tim* stories. Loughborough: Ladybird.

Ahlberg, J. and A. (1981) *Peepo!* London: Puffin.

Allen, P. (1980) *Mr Archimedes' Bath.* London: Puffin.

Armitage, R. and D. (1992) *When Dad Did the Washing.* London: Puffin.

Ashley, B. (1992) *Clever Sticks.* London: Picture Lions.

Bailey, P. (1993) *Scarey Story.* London: Picture Hippo.

Burningham, J. (1978) *Time to Get Out of the Bath Shirley.* London: Random House.

Coventry Education Department, (undated) *The Chinese New Year Story Book.* Minority Service, Southfield Old School, South Street, Coventry CV1 SEJ.

Field, S. (1990) *J.J. and the Washing Machines.* Hove: Firefly.

Garland, S. (1995) *Coming to Tea.* London: Puffin.

Garland, S. (2003) *Doing the Washing.* London: Puffin.

Gray, K. and Sharratt, N. (2001) *Eat Your Peas.* London: Red Fox.

Hayes, S. (1988) *Eat Up Gemma.* London: Walker Books.

Hayes, S. (1996) *Gemma's First Christmas.* London: Walker Books.

Hedderwick, M. (1994) *Oh No! Peebie Peebles.* London: Red Fox.

Hewett, A. (1966) *Mrs Mopple's Washing Line.* London: Red Fox.

Hughes, S. (1978) *Moving Molly.* London: Picture Lions.

Manning, M. and Granstom, B. (2000) *Wash, Scrub and Brush.* London: Franklin Watts.
Mascurel, C. (2001) *Two Homes.* London: Walker Books.
Miller, V. (1992) *Eat Your Dinner.* London: Walker Books.
Mitton, T. and Million, L. (2000) *What's the Time Mr Wolf?* London: Walker Books.
Murphy, J. (1980) *Peace at Last.* London: Picture Mac.
Ross, T. (1998) *I Don't Want a Bath.* London: Collins.
Ross, T. (2003) *I Don't Want to Wash My Hands.* London: Picture Lions.
Smith, L. (1995) *Dat's New Year (Celebrations series).* London: A. & C. Black.
Thomas, V. and Korky, P. (1987) *Winnie the Witch.* Oxford: OUP.
Ward, N. (2002) *A Wolf at the Door.* London: Scholastic.
Wildsmith, B. (1989) *The Christmas Story.* Oxford: OUP.

CD-ROM

SEMERC Microworlds 2000. London: Granada Learning Ltd.

Music

Harrop, B. (1975) (Ed.) *Apusskidu Songs for Children.* London: A. & C. Black.
'I jump out of bed in the morning',
McGregor, H. (2000) *Bingo Lingo.* London: A. & C. Black.
'No room'.
Okki-tokki-unga Action Songs for Children. Harrop, B. (Ed.) (1978) London: A. & C. Black.
'Someone's in the kitchen with Dinah'.
'Ten in a bed'.
'The wise man and the foolish man'.

Health care

Optician's

Non-fiction

Amery, H. (1998) *Children's Bible.* London: Usborne.
Boots Opticians (1991) *'Katy Visits an Optician'.*

Fiction

Boucher, C. and Merriman, R. (1999) *The Six Blind Men and the Elephant.* London: Walker Books.
Cousins, L. (1991) *What Can Pinky See?* London: Walker Books.
Leaflets about eyes from the optician's.

Dentist's

Adamson, J. and G. (2003) *Topsy and Tim Go to the Dentist.* Loughborough: Ladybird.
Civardi, A. and Cartwright, S. (2000) First Experiences series. *Going to the Dentist.* London: Usborne.
Cunliffe, J. (1989) *Postman Pat's Sore Tooth.* London: Hippo Scholastic.
Groves, P. (1999) *Bangers and Mash Toothday and Birthday.* Harlow: Longman.
Leaflets from the dentist's.
Moss, M. and Mocleler, J. (2001) *Wibble Wobble.* London: Orchard.
Ross, T. (2002) *Teeth.* London: Anderson Press.

Music

Sanderson, A. (1997) *Me Songs plus CD for 4–7 year olds.*
'All I want for Christmas is my two front teeth'. London: A. & C. Black.

Doctor's

Non-fiction

Amery, H. (1998) *Children's Bible.* London: Usborne.
Cartwright, S. and Civardi, A. (2000) Usborne First Experiences: *Going to the Doctor.* London: Usborne.
Cartwright, S. and Civardi, A. (2002) Usborne First Experiences: *Going to the Hospital.* London: Usborne.
Mercer, G. (1988) *Stepping Stones Inside a Hospital.* London: Kingfisher.
Royston, A. (1995) *Getting Better.* London: Francis Lincoln.
Wood, T. (1989) My Job series: *The Ambulance Driver.* London: Franklin Watts.
Wood, T. (1989) My Job series: *The Doctor.* London: Franklin Watts.
Wood, T. (1989) My Job series: *The Nurse.* London: Franklin Watts.

Fiction

Adamson, J. and A. (1997) *Topsy and Tim and the Big Surprise.* Loughborough: Ladybird.
Adamson, J. and A. (1999) *Topsy and Tim Go to Hospital.* Loughborough: Ladybird.
Adamson, J. and G. (1999) *Topsy and Tim Meet the Ambulance Crew.* Loughborough: Ladybird.
Adamson, J. and G. (2003) *Topsy and Tim and the New Baby.* Loughborough: Ladybird.
Adamson, J. and G. (2003) *Topsy and Tim Go to the Doctor.* Loughborough: Ladybird.
Ahlberg, A. and Jaques, F. (1981) *Miss Dose the Doctor's Daughter.* London: Puffin.
Ahlberg, J. and A. (1980) *Funny Bones.* London: Picture Lions.
Ahlberg, J. and A. (1991) *Bye Bye Baby.* London: Little Mammoth.
Anholt, L. and C. (1995) *Sophie and the New Baby.* London: Orchard.

Civardi, A. and Cartwright, S. (2000) First Experiences: *Going to the Doctor.* London: Usborne.
Civardi, A. and Cartwright, S. (2000) First Experiences: *Going to Hospital.* London: Usborne.
Civardi, A. and Cartwright, S. (2000) First Experiences: *New Baby.* London: Usborne.
Hawkins, C.J. (1987) *Foxy and the Spots.* London: Orchard.
Ross, T. (2000) *I Don't Want to Go to Hospital.* London: Anderson Press.

Music

Harrop, B. (Ed.) (1978) *Okki-tokki-unga Action Songs for Children.* London: A. & C. Black.
Harrop, B. (Ed.) (1975) *Apusskidu Songs for Children* London: A. & C. Black.
Sanderson, A. (1997) *Me Songs plus CD for 4–7 year olds.* London: A. & C. Black.

CD-ROM

At the Doctor's and My World: Faces, Bodies London: Granada Learning.

Shops and services

Sports centre

Bolam, E. and Parker, V. (1996) *Bearobics.* London: Hodder.
Butterworth, N. (1996) *Sports Day*. London: Hodder.
Cooke, T. (2000) *Zoom.* London: Collins.
Garland, S. (1996) *Going Swimming.* London: Puffin.
Kubler, A. (1995) *Come Play with Us.* Swindon: Child's Play International.
Newcome, Z. (1996) *Toddlerobics.* London: Walker Books.
Rosen, M. and Oxenbury, H. (1993) *We're Going on a Bear Hunt.* London: Walker Books.
Simons, F. and Winter, S. (1998) *Calling All Toddlers.* London: Orion.
Tilden, R. (1995) *Keep Fit Froggy.* London: Orion.

Greengrocer's

Non-fiction

Bastyra, J. (1995) *Get Set Fruit.* London: Watts Books.
Bastyra, J. (1995) *Get Set Vegetables.* London: Watts Books.
Burningham, J. (1980) *The Shopping List.* London: Red Fox.
Lynn, S. and James, D. (1992) *Why We Eat.* London: Two-Can.
Oxfam (1995) *Come Eat With Us.* Swindon: Child's Play International.

Fiction

Adamson, A. and J. (1999) *Topsy and Tim Little Shoppers.* Loughborough: Ladybird.
Brown, E. (1994) *Handa's Surprise.* London: Walker Books.
Burningham, J. (1980) *The Shopping Basket.* London: Red Fox.
Burningham, J. (1982) *Avocado Baby.* London: Picture Lions.
Child, L. (2000) *Will Not Ever Never Eat a Tomato.* London: Orchard.
French, V. (1995) *Oliver's Vegetables.* London: Hodder.
French, V. (1998) *Oliver's Fruit Salad.* London: Hodder.
French, V. and Ayliffe, A. (2000) *Let's Go Anna.* London: Gullane Children's Books.
Garland, S. (1995) *Going Shopping.* London: Puffin.
Garland, S. (1996) *Doing the Garden.* London: Puffin.
Graham-Yooll, L. (1995) *Grandpa's Garden.* Andover: Ragged Bears.
Hughes, M. and Forsythe, A. (1999) *Stone Soup.* Oxford: Ginn.
Laird, E. (1999) *King of the Supermarket.* London: Hippo.
Lodge, J. (2000) *Going Shopping.* London: Campbell Books.
Ross, T. (1987) *Stone Soup.* London: Picture Lions.
Scarry, R. (1969) *The Supermarket.* London: Picture Lions.
Tolstoy, A. and Sharkey, N. (1999) *The Gigantic Turnip.* London: Barefoot.

CD-ROM

My World: Sorting (fruit).

Music

Harrop, B. (Ed.) (1975) *Apusskidu Songs for Children.* London: A. & C. Black.
MacGregor (1998) *Tom Thumb's Musical Maths.* London: A. & C. Black.
Harrop, B. (Ed.) (1978) *Okki-tokki-unga Action Songs for Children.* London: A. & C. Black.

Post office

Non-fiction

Alexander, J. (2000) *A Better Letter.* Harlow: Longman-Pearson Education.
Alexander, J. (2000) *Addressing a Letter.* Harlow: Longman-Pearson Education.
Alexander, J. (2000) *Pip's Thankyou Letter.* Harlow: Longman-Pearson Education.
Alexander, J. (2000) *Postcards.* Harlow: Longman-Pearson Education.
Wood, T. (1989) My Job series: *The Post Woman.* London: Franklin Watts.

Fiction

Ahlberg, J. and A. (1996) *Jolly Postman* books. London: Heinemann.

Campbell, R. (1988) *My Presents.* London: Macmillan.
Cunliffe, J. *Postman Pat Stories.* London: Hippo.
Dodd, M. and Richardson, J. (1993) *The Lost Doll.* London: Puffin.
Hawkins, C. and J. (1997) *Numberlies.* London: Dorling Kindersley.
H. O. Ross, T. (1997) *A Message for Santa.* London: Collins.

Music

Nicholls, S. (1992) *Bobby Shaftoe Clap Your Hands.* London: A. & C. Black.
  'Postman's Knocking'.

B & Q Warehouse

Non-fiction

Amerylt (1998) *Children's Bible.* London Usborne (story: The Wise Man Built
  His House on the Rocks).
Chapman, G. (1988) *Machines at Work: Building Works.* London: Walker Books.
Jackman, W. (1991) *My Book About Houses and Homes.* Hove: Wayland.
Kubler, A. (1995) *Come Home with Us.* Swindon: Child's Play International.

Fiction

Adamson, A. and J. (1997) *Topsy and Tim: The Busy Builders.* Loughborough:
  Ladybird.
Ahlberg, A. (1981) *Miss Brick the Builder's Daughter.* London: Puffin.
Ahlberg, J. and A. (1981) *Peepo!* London: Puffin.
Baxter, N. (2000) *The Trouble with Tippers.* Menai Bridge: Bookmark Ltd.
Fogden, E. (2001) *The House that Bob Built* and other *Bob the Builder* books and
  videos. London: BBC Worldwide Ltd.
Gale, C. (2001) *Bob and Eddie Paint the House.* London: Little Hippo.
Hedderwick, M. (1994) *Oh No! Peedie Peebles.* London: Red Fox.
Imai, M. (1994) *Little Lumpty.* London: Walker Books.
Mayo, D. (1950) *The House that Jack Built.* Loughborough: Ladybird.
Thomas, V. (1987) *Winnie the Witch.* Oxford: Oxford University Press.
Waddell, M. (1993) *Baby Hammer.* London: Walker Books.
Wallace, J. (1997) *Building a House with Mr Bumble.* London: Walker Books.

Music

Davies, N. (1999) *Music: The Literacy Connection.* Greenfield Music, PO Box
  117, Lancaster, LA1 1WY. (Song 'Jen the Hen').
Harrop, B. (Ed.) (1975) *Apusskidu Songs for children.* London: A. & C. Black.
Harrop, B. (Ed.) (1978) *Okki-tokki-unga Action Songs for Children.* London:
  A. & C. Black.
'Peter Hammers with One Hammer'.
'The Wise Man Built his House Upon the Rocks'.

Cafe

Non-fiction

Bastyra, J. (1995) *Bread.* London: Watts.
Bastyra, J. (1995) *Cheese.* London: Watts.
Bastyra, J. (1995) *Fruit.* London: Watts.
Bastyra, J. (1995) *Vegetables.* London: Watts.
Various cookbooks and non-fiction food books.

Fiction

Ahlberg, A. and J. (1980) *Mrs Wobble the Waitress.* London: Puffin.
Ashley, B. (1992) *Cleversticks.* Picture Lions
Boon, D. (1998) *Gio's Pizzas.* Hove: MacDonald Young.
Dowling, P. (1998) *Beans on Toast.* London: Walker.
Hawkins, C. and J. (1997) *Max and the School Dinners.* London: Puffin.
Jackman, W. (1991) *My Book About Food.* London: Wayland.
James, D. and Lynn, S. (1992) *What Can We Eat?* London: Two-Can.
Kubler, A. (1996) *Come Eat with Us.* Swindon: Child's Play International.
Mathias and Thomson (1988) *A to Z Food.* London: Franklin Watts.
Miller, V. (1992) *Eat Your Dinner.* London: Walker Books.
Pelham, D. (1990) *Sam's Sandwich.* London: Jonathan Cape.
Sharratt, N. (1994) *Ketchup on Your Cornflakes.* London: Scholastic.
Sharratt, N. (1996) *A Cheese and Tomato Spider.* London: Scholastic.
Sharratt, N. (2000) *Don't Put Your Finger in the Jelly Nelly!* London: Scholastic.

CD-ROM

At The Café Granada Learning.

Music

Harrop, B. (Ed.) (1975) *Apusskidu Songs for Children.* London: A. & C. Black.
Harrop, B. (Ed.) (1978) *Okki-tokki-unga Action Songs for Children.* London: A. & C. Black.
'I jump out of bed in the morning'
MacGregor (1998) *Tom Thumb's Musical Maths* London: A. & C. Black.
McGregor, H. (2000) *Bingo Lingo.* London: A. & C. Black.
'No room'
Sanderson, A. (1997) *Me* London: A. & C. Black.
'Sweet Potato',
'I'm So Hot. Food wrap'.
'Jelly belly'.

Vet's surgery, pet shop and zoo

Non-fiction

Amos, J. (1993) *Animal Index: Ponds and streams.* Beckerton, Somerset: Emma Books Ltd.
Amos, J. (1993) *Animal Index: Pets.* Beckerton, Somerset: Emma Books Ltd.
Amos, J. (1993) *Animal Index: Pets On the Farm.* Beckerton, Somerset: Emma Books Ltd.
Amos, J. (1993) *Animal Index: Woods and Fields.* Beckerton, Somerset: Emma Books Ltd.
Axworthy, A. (1999) Peep-hole books: *Guess What I Am.* London: Walker Books.
Axworthy, A. (1999) Peep-hole books: *Guess Where I Live.* London Walker Books.
Axworthy, A. (1999) Peep-hole books: *Guess Who My Mummy Is.* London: Walker Books.
Axworthy, A. (1999) Peep-hole books: *What I'll Like.* London: Walker Books.
Butterfield, M. (1999) *Zoo Animals.* Loughborough: Ladybird.
Campbell, R. (1982) *Dear Zoo.* London: Puffin.
Campbell, R. (1996) *ABC Zoo.* London: Campbell books.
Civardi, A. and Cartwright, S. (2000) *The New Puppy.* London: Usborne.
Collins, R. (2000) Who am I series: *I Live in the Jungle.* London: Franklin Watts.
Mettler, R. Jeunesse, G. (1993) First Discovery: *The Jungle.* Moonlight Publishing.
Pluckrose, H. (1989) Look At series: *Fur and Feathers.* London: Franklin Watts.
Pluckrose, H. (1989) Look At series: *Paws and Claws.* London: Franklin Watts.
Pluckrose, H. (1989) Look At series: *Skin, Shell and Scales.* London: Franklin Watts.
Pluckrose, H. (1989) Look At series: *Teeth and Tusks.* London: Franklin Watts.
Watts, C. (1991) Jump Start Book: *On Safari.* London: Two-Can.
Watts, C. (1991) Jump Start Book: *Pets.* London: Two-Can.
Wood, T. (1989) My Job series: *The Vet.* London: Franklin Watts.

Fiction

Adamson, J. and A. (1997) *Topsy and Tim and the Lost Rabbit.* Loughborough: Ladybird.
Adamson, J. and A. (1998) *Topsy and Tim and the New Puppy.* Loughborough: Ladybird.
Adamson, J. and A. (1998) *Topsy and Tim Go to the Zoo.* Loughborough: Ladybird.
Adamson, J. and A. (2003) *Topsy and Tim at the Farm.* Loughborough: Ladybird.
Adamson, J. and A. (2003) *Topsy and Tim Look after Pets.* Loughborough: Ladybird.
Andreae, G. and Wojtowiycz, D. (1998) *Rumble in the Jungle.* London: Orchard.
Harter, D. (2000) *The Animal Boogie.* Bristol: Barefoot.
Hepburn, M. (2001) *Animal Hospital stories Kooky the Kitten.* London: BBC.
Hepburn, M. (2001) *Animal Hospital stories Patch the puppy.* London: BBC.
Hepburn, M. (2001) *Animal Hospital stories Pepper the Pony.* London: BBC.

Kavanagh, P. (1997) *The Three Little Guinea Pigs*. London: Little Hippo.
Keer, J. (1966) *Mog Visits the Vet's*. London: Collins.
Moore, I. (1991) *Six Dinner Sid*. Hemel Hempstead: Simon and Schuster.
Palma Dalla (1991) *Zoo Hullaballoo*. Hayes Middlesex: Magi.
Wilson, A. and Bartlett (1999) *Over the Grasslands*. London: Macmillan.

CD-ROM

At the Vets, *Fetch the Vets*. London: Granada Learning.

Music

Harrop, B. (Ed.) (1975) *Apusskidu Songs for Children*. London: A. & C. Black.
Harrop, B. (Ed.) (1978) *Okki-tokki-unga Action Songs for Children*. London: A. & C. Black.
'The animals went in two by two',
'Going to the zoo',
'Daddy wouldn't buy me a Bow-wow'.
MacGregor (1998) *Tom Thumb's Musical Maths*. London: A. & C. Black.
MacGregor (1999) *Bingo Lingo*. London: A. & C. Black.
'One Elephant'.
Silver Burdett Music Scheme Level One–Listen to Carnival of the Animals (tape 3A)

Transport and journeys

Kubler, A. and Formby, C. (1995) *Come Ride With Us*. Swindon: Child's Play International.
Tong, W. and Cummins, J. (1997) *Cars, Boats, Trains and Planes*. London: Harper Collins.

Cars, lorries or bicycles

Adamson, J. and A. (1998) *Topsy and Tim Have New Bikes*. Loughborough Ladybird.
Burningham, J. (1973) *Mr Gumpy's Motor Car*. London: Red Fox.
Grant, G. (1991) *The Little Blue Car*. London: Orchard.

Train

Amery, H. and Cartwright, S. (1999) *Train Stories*. London: Usborne.
Awdry, W.V. (2002) *Thomas and Friends*. London: Heinemann Young Books.
Burningham, J. (1999) *Oi! Get Off the Train* London: Red Fox.
Crebbin, J. (1996) *The Train Ride*. London: Walker Books.

McAllister, A. and Curless, A. (1995) *Daniel's Trains*. London: Random House.
Mitton, T. and Parker, A. (1998) *Terrific Trains*. London: Kingfisher.
Wormell, C. (2000) *The Animal Train*. London: Jonathan Cape.

Bus and coach

Hindley, J. (1995) *The Big Red Bus*. London: Walker Books.
Ruth, C. (2002) *The School Bus*. Cheshire: Cheshire Studio.
Zelinsky, P.O. (2000) *The Wheels on the Bus*. London: Orchard Books.

Aeroplane

Adamson, J. and A. (1998) *Topsy and Tim Go on an Aeroplane*. Loughborough: Ladybird.
Gutterman, A. (2000) *Lily Goes on a Plane*. London: Franklin Watts.
McPhail, D. (1999) *My First Flight*. Bradfield Essex: Happy Cat Books.
Milton, T. and Parker, A. (1998) *Amazing Planes*. London: Kingfisher.

Rocket

Foreman, M. (1993) *Dinosaurs and All That Rubbish*. London: Puffin.
Milton, T. and Parker, A. (1998) *Roaring Rockets*. London: Kingfisher.
Murphy, J. (1995) *Whatever Next*. London: Macmillan.
Pienkowski, H. and J. (1994) *Meg and Mog (Meg on the Moon)*. London: Puffin.
Sharratt, N. (1995) *Countdown*. London: Walker Books.

Boats and water

Books

Non-fiction

Amerylt (1998) *Children's Bible*. London: Usborne.
Fowler, R. (1986) *My Noisy Little Boat*. London: Mammoth.
James, D. and Lynn, S. (1992) *A Jump Start Book Underwater*. London: Scholastic.
Mitton and Parker (2002) *Brilliant Boats*. London: Kingfisher.

Fiction

Alborough, J. (2003) *Captain Duck*. London: Collins.
Allen, P. (1982) *Who Sank the Boat*. London: Puffin.
Beck, I. (1995) *The Owl and the Pussy-cat by Edward Lear*. London: Picture Corgi.
Blathway, B. (1996) *Bellac Goes To Sea*. London: Random House.
Cain, S. and Linch, T. (1998) *Look Out for the Big Fish*. London: Magi.

Giles, A. and Wojtowycz, D. (1999) *Commotion in the Ocean.* London: Orchard Books.

Goodhart, P. (1997) *Row, Row, Row Your Boat.* London: Heinemann.

Grindley, S. (2001) *Don't Rock the Boat.* London: Dorling Kindersley.

Kennaway, A. (1990) *Curious Clownfish.* London: Frances Lincoln.

Krasilovsky, P. (1970) *The Cow Fell in the Canal.* London: Puffin.

Mayher, J. (1997) *Shelley Silvertail the Mermaid.* London: Orion.

Munoz, C. (1995) *Little Captain.* London: Red Fox.

Pfister, M. (1992) *The Rainbow Fish.* London: North South Books.

Scarry, R. (1995) *Busy Town Regatta.* London: Collins.

Sendak, M. (2000) *Where the Wild Things Are.* London: Puffin.

Snape, C. and J. (1990) *Busy Day.* London: Walker Books.

Music books

Harrop, B. (1975) *Apusskidu Songs for children.* London: A. & C. Black. 'Yellow submarine'; 'My ship sailed from China'.

Harrop, B. (1978) *Okki-tokki-unga Action Songs for Children.* London: A. & C. Black.

Roberts, J. (1989) *Music Book 1 (4–7s)* (Silver Burdett and Ginn Music). Morristown ,NJ, 'A sailor went to sea'; 'The big ship sails on the alley alley oh', 'Row row row your boat'; 'Weather effects'.

Music

Harrop, B. (Ed.) (1975) *Apusskidu Songs for Children.* London: A. & C. Black.

Harrop, B. (Ed.) (1978) *Okki-tokki-unga Action Songs for Children.* London: A. & C. Black.

MacGregor (1999) *Bingo Lingo.* London: A. & C. Black.

MacGregor (1998) *Tom Thumb's Musical Maths.* London: A. & C. Black.

Umansky, K. (2000) *Three Tapping Teddies* London: A. & C. Black.

Familiar Stories

The Three Bears

Hunia, F. (1997) *Goldilocks and the Three Bears.* Loughborough: Ladybird.

MacDonald, A. and Williamson G. (1998) *Beware of the Bears.* London: Magi.

Marshall, J. (1990) *Goldilocks and the Three Bears.* London: Picture Lions.

Stevenson, P. (1997) *Goldilocks and the Three Bears' Puppet Theatre.* Haydock St. Helens: Ted Smart.

Ward, N. (2003) *Who's Been Eating My Porridge.* London: Scholastic.

Other bear stories

Alborough, J. (1992) *Where's my Teddy?* London: Walker Books.
Beck, I. (1989) *The Teddy Bear Robber.* London: Doubleday.
Hissey, J. (2000) Old Bear series. London: Red Fox.
Waddel, M. (1980) *Peace At Last.* London: Macmillan.

Non-fiction

Hoshino, M. *The Grizzly Bear Family*, and other books about wild bears. North South books.

Music

Harrop, B. (Ed.) (1975) *Apusskidu Songs for Children.* London: A. & C. Black. 'The bear went over the mountain'.
Davies, N. (1999) *Music: The Literacy Connection.* 'Goldilocks'.
MacGregor (1998) *Tom Thumb's Musical Maths.* London: A. & C. Black.
Harrop, B. (Ed.) (1978) *Okki-tokki-unga Action Songs for Children.* London: A. & C. Black.
'The Three Bears'
'The Teddy Bears Picnic' music.
Umansky, K. *Three Tapping Teddies.* London A. & C. Black
'Goldilocks' Tale'.

CD-ROM

My World – Dress Teddy and the Three Bears.

Snow White

Disney (1991) *Disney Easy Reader: Snow White and the Seven Dwarfs.* Disney Classic Films.
Sibley, R. and Aitchison (1993) *Old Favourite Tales. Snow White and the Seven Dwarfs.* Loughborough: Ladybird.
Snow White. Loughborough: Ladybird.

The Three Little Pigs

Mitton, T. (2000) *What's the Time Mr Wolf?* London: Early Learning Centre.
Rayner, M. (1994) *One By One Garth Pig's Rain Song.* London: Macmillan.
Trivizas, E. and Oxenbury, H. (1995) *Three Little Wolves and the Big Bad Pig.* London: Heinemann.
The Three Little Pigs Story and songs
Umansky, K. (1994) *Three Singing Pigs.* London: A. & C. Black.
Ward, N. (2002) *A Wolf at my Door.* London: Scholastic.
Non-fiction books about wolves and pigs in the wild and on farms.

CD-ROM

Hawker, J. (1997) *Walk with a Wolf.* London: Walker Books.
The Three Little Pigs (CD-Rom) (code 420001) from AVP School Centre, Chepstow, Monmouthshire, NP16 5PH.

Music

Mac Gregor (1999) *Bingo Lingo.*
'Huff puff': A. & C. Black.

The Three Billy Goats Gruff

Carpenter, S. (1998) *Three Billy Goats Gruff.* London: Harper Collins.
Finch, M. (2001) *The Three Billy Goats Gruff.* Bristol: Barefoot Books.
Hastings, E. (1995) *The Three Billy Goats Gruff.* London: Greenwich Education.
Langley, J. (1991) *The Three Billy Goats Gruff.* London: Picture Lions.
Three Billy Goats Gruff. Loughborough: Ladybird.
Umansky, K. (1994) *Three Singing Pigs.* London: A. & C. Black.
Wade, B. (2001) *Three Billy Goats Gruff.* London: Franklin Watts.

Red Riding Hood

Amos, J. (1993) *Animal Index Woods and Fields* Beckerton Somerset: Emma Books Ltd.
Hawker, J. (1997) *Walk with a Wolf.* London: Walker Books.
Non-fiction books about flowers and woodlands.

Fiction

Cartwright, S. (1987) *First Stories: Little Red Riding Hood.* London: Usborne.
Cartwright, S. Amery, H. (1998) *First Fairy Stories: Red Riding Hood.* London: Usborne.
Cullimore (1998) *Red Riding Hood.* London: Longman.
Grim, J. (1993) *Little Red Riding Hood.* Loughborough: Ladybird.
Langley, J. (1997) *Little Red Riding Hood.* London: Collins.
Mitto, T. (2000) *Little Red Riding Hood Pop-Up Book.* London: Walker Books.
Mitton, T. and Million, L. (2000) *What's the Time Mr Wolf?* London: Walker Books.
Sharratt, N. (2000) *Little Red Riding Hood. A Lift Flap Fairy Tale.* London: Scholastic.
Stevenson, P. (1997) *Little Red Riding Hood.* Haydock St. Helens: Ted Smart.
Umansky, K. (2000) *Three Tapping Teddies* London: A. & C. Black.
Songs about Little Red Riding Hood
Ward, N. (2002) *A Wolf at the Door.* London: Scholastic.

Music

Bryant, A. (2001) *Mister Wolf and Little Red Riding Hood* (published by Golden Apple Productions, London).

186

BIBLIOGRAPHY

Bruce, T. (1991) *Time to Play in the Early Years*. London: Hodder & Stoughton.

Bruce, T. (2001) *Learning Through Play*. London: Hodder & Stoughton.

Cousins, J. (1999) *Listening to Four Year Olds*. The National Early Years Network.

Duffy, B. (1998) *Supporting Creativity and Imagination in the Early Years*. Oxford: OUP.

Ensing, J. and Spencer, B. (2001) *Children Learning Communication, Language and Literacy*. Spencer.

Ensing, J. and Spencer, B. (2002) *Children Learning Personal, Social and Emotional Development*. Spencer.

Hall, N. and Young *Being in Role*. Reading University.

Hendy, L. and Toon, L. (2001) *Supporting Drama and Imaginative Play in the Early Years*.

Hutchin, V. (1996) *Tracking Achievement in Early Years*. London: Hodder & Stoughton.

Liverpool Early Years Development Team (2000) *Learning Intentions for the Foundation Stage Curriculum*.

Moyles, J. (1998) *The Excellence of Play*. Oxford: OUP.

O'Connel, B. and Bretherton, I. (1984), *Symbolic Play: The development of social understanding*. New York: Academic.

QCA (2000) *Curriculum Guidance for the Foundation Stage* (Ref: QCA/00/587). London: QCA/DfEE.

QCA (2003) *Foundation Stage Profiles and Handbook* and *Foundation Stage Booklet* (Ref: QCA/03/1006). London: QCA/DfEE.

Smith, P. (1999) *Understanding Children's Development*. London: Blackwell Learning.

Toye, N. and Prendiville, F. (2000) *Drama and Traditional Story in the Early Years*. London: Routledge Falmer.

Wood, E. and Attfield, J. (1996) *Play Learning and the Early Childhood Experience* London: Paul Chapman.

Other useful resource books and magazines

Amery, H. (1998) *Bible Stories* London: Usborne.

Griffiths, N. (2001) *A Corner to Learn*. Cheltenham: Nelson-Thornes Ltd.

Harrison, L.S. (1988) *Dance and Drama*. London: Scholastic.

Nursery Education Magazine. London: Scholastic. Monthly subscriptions Tel: 01926 816250.

Music books

Davies, N. *The Literacy Connection* (a musical/literacy package) obtained from The Literacy Connection, Greenfield Music, PO Box 117, Lancaster LAI IWY.

Harrop, B. (ed.) (1976) *Okki-tokki-unga Action Songs for Children with double cassette.* London: A. & C. Black.

Harrop, B. (ed.) (1996) *Apusskidu: Songs for Children.* London: A. & C. Black.

MacGregor, H. (1992) *Tom Thumb's Musical Maths.* London: A. & C. Black.

MacGregor, H. (1999) *Bingo Lingo.* London: A. & C. Black.

Nicholls, S. (1992) *Bobby Shaftoe Clap Your Hands.* London: A. & C. Black.

Sanderson, A. (1997) *Me Songs plus CD for 4–7 year-olds.* London: A. & C. Black.

Silver Burdett & Ginn Music Book 1 (4–7 year-olds) (1989) Cheltenham: Nelson Thornes Ltd.

Umansky, K. (1994) *Three Singing Pigs.* London: A. & C. Black.

Umansky, K. (1998) *Three Rapping Rats.* London: A. & C. Black.

Umansky, K. (2000) *Three Tapping Teddies.* London: A. & C. Black.